WHEN

MAN

BEGAN

TO CALL

ON GOD

T. W. HUNT

WHEN MAN BEGAN TO CALL ON GOD

A BRIEF HISTORY *of* PRAYER *in the* BIBLE

NAVPRESS

Discipleship Inside Out®

Discipleship Inside Out®

NavPress is the publishing ministry of The Navigators, an international Christian organization and leader in personal spiritual development. NavPress is committed to helping people grow spiritually and enjoy lives of meaning and hope through personal and group resources that are biblically rooted, culturally relevant, and highly practical.

For a free catalog go to www.NavPress.com
or call 1.800.366.7788 in the United States or 1.800.839.4769 in Canada.

ISBN-13: 978-1-61747-993-9

Cover design by Arvid Wallen

Some of the anecdotal illustrations in this book are true to life and are included with the permission of the persons involved. All other illustrations are composites of real situations, and any resemblance to people living or dead is coincidental.

Unless otherwise identified, all Scripture quotations in this publication are taken from The Holy Bible, English Standard Version (ESV), copyright © 2001 by Crossway Bibles, a division of Good News Publishers. Used by permission. All rights reserved. Other versions used include: the Holman Christian Standard Bible (HCSB)® Copyright © 2003, 2002, 2000, 1999 by Holman Bible Publishers. All rights reserved.

Hunt, T. W., 1929-
  When man began to call on God : a brief history of prayer in the Bible / T.W. Hunt.
    pages cm
  Includes bibliographical references.
  ISBN 978-1-61747-993-9
  1. Prayer—Biblical teaching. 2. Bible—Criticism, interpretation, etc. I. Title.
  BS680.P64H87 2013
  248.3'2—dc23
                                2013006375

Printed in the United States of America

1 2 3 4 5 6 7 8 / 18 17 16 15 14 13

To Melana Hunt Monroe,
who helped God make my prayers worth the effort. Her
proofreading, suggestions, and insights were significant,
and her influence on this book was incomparable.

CONTENTS

Introduction: With God All Things Are Possible   9

Chapter 1:   Genesis   13

Chapter 2:   Exodus   21

Chapter 3:   Leviticus, Numbers, Deuteronomy   27

Chapter 4:   Joshua, Judges, Ruth   37

Chapter 5:   Samuel, Kings, Chronicles   47

Chapter 6:   Ezra, Nehemiah, Esther, Job   67

Chapter 7:   Psalms, Proverbs, Ecclesiastes, Song of Solomon   77

Chapter 8:   Isaiah, Jeremiah, Lamentations   93

Chapter 9:   Ezekiel, Daniel   105

Chapter 10:   Hosea Through Malachi   111

Chapter 11:   Matthew, Mark   127

Chapter 12:   Luke   143

Chapter 13:   John   153

Chapter 14:   Acts   163

Chapter 15:   Romans, Corinthians   171

Chapter 16:   Galatians Through Philemon   183

Chapter 17:   Hebrews Through Jude   195

Chapter 18:   Revelation   205

Appendix: All the Prayers of the Bible   213

Notes   225

About the Author   227

H. Alderman

Mr. & Mrs. Leon Alderman
1272 Mapleview Street S.E.
Grand Rapids, MI 49508

Introduction

WITH GOD ALL THINGS ARE POSSIBLE

God's Word is saturated with prayer, containing almost a thousand prayers or passages on prayer. Prayers are offered for consolation and assurance in every conceivable kind of circumstance. The young offered prayer, as did the elderly, the terrified, the happy, the despairing, the grateful, the penitent, prophets, kings, priests, the sick, and many more men and women. At times, prayers are expressed in exquisite poetry, at times in prose, and at times plaintive, but all the Bible's prayers fit our human condition and can help us find our way to God today. This book traces the development of prayer in the Bible as God gradually unfolded His plan for relationship with humans through their prayers.

Genesis 18:14 is the key prayer verse for all of the Bible as it typifies the many occasions when Scripture tells us that nothing is impossible with God.

> Is anything too hard for the LORD? At the appointed time I will return to you, about this time next year, and Sarah shall have a son.

Repeatedly, the Bible assures us of God's unlimited power. After Moses' prayer for meat for the wandering nation, God encouraged him,

"Is the LORD's hand shortened? Now you shall see whether my word will come true for you or not" (Numbers 11:23).

After God's revelation of His enormous power to Job, Job answered, "I know that you can do all things, and that no purpose of yours can be thwarted" (Job 42:2). When the Lord prompted Jeremiah to purchase Hanamel's field as an assurance that He Himself would preserve the property in perpetuity, Jeremiah's faith declared, "Ah, Lord GOD! It is you who have made the heavens and the earth by your great power and by your outstretched arm! Nothing is too hard for you" (Jeremiah 32:17).

The Lord Himself backed Jeremiah's faith by stating (in connection with ultimate restoration of the land after it was conquered by the Chaldeans), "Behold, I am the LORD, the God of all flesh. Is anything too hard for me?" (Jeremiah 32:27). Some time later, God guaranteed to Zechariah the return of the land to the Israelite nation: "If it is marvelous in the sight of the remnant of this people in those days, should it also be marvelous in my sight, declares the LORD of hosts?" (Zechariah 8:6-7).

This faith in God's omnipotence recurs in the New Testament. The warning of John the Baptist to the Pharisees and Sadducees was, "And do not presume to say to yourselves, 'We have Abraham as our father,' for I tell you, God is able from these stones to raise up children for Abraham" (Matthew 3:9).

When Mary questioned Gabriel about bearing a son virginally, Gabriel told her, "And behold, your relative Elizabeth in her old age has also conceived a son, and this is the sixth month with her who was called barren. For nothing will be impossible with God" (Luke 1:36-37).

Jesus Himself joined these affirmations by informing the disciples that the rich could overcome their greed and enter the kingdom of heaven. He told them, "With man this is impossible, but with God all things are possible" (Matthew 19:26).

Paul's doxology later stated,

Now to him who is able to do far more abundantly than all that we ask or think, according to the power at work within us, to him be glory in the church and in Christ Jesus throughout all generations, forever and ever. Amen. (Ephesians 3:20-21)

This imperative to believe in God's power was obligatory throughout the Bible as person after person needed the assurance of God's omnipotence, especially in his or her prayers. True faith is impossible if we do not believe God is omnipotent.

ABOUT THIS BOOK

When I began my investigation into prayer, I started with Genesis, and, book by book, worked my way through the Bible, searching for major prayer themes. Certain verses struck me as being key, and I identified these for each book, along with its major prayer theme(s). The key verse gives us an important aspect of prayer; the key theme summarizes the main instances of prayer in the book. The key prayer verse does not always coincide with the book's major concepts, but is important to a biblical understanding of prayer.

I made no effort to arrange the material chronologically, but simply followed the biblical order. The overall result is in a rough chronology, and that arrangement corresponds to my personal growth in prayer over the years! For example, the earliest mention of prayer is "calling" on God, or invoking Him, which little children do, even if they do not understand the concept. The main theme in Exodus is crying to God, which every Christian experiences early in his or her walk. I certainly did!

The chapter divisions in this book are somewhat topical. I placed books of the Kings together, while Genesis, with its introductions to many kinds of prayer, has its own chapter. Exodus, with the theme of crying to God, has its own chapter because of the large number of other occasions when a pray-er cried to God. Because it also seemed more readable, I placed together many of the shorter books of the Bible.

Remember that this book touches only *prayer*. It is not a commentary on the books of the Bible. Many major biblical details and incidents are omitted in the attempt to keep the reader's attention on prayer.[1] This book is primarily a history; this allows readers to draw their own conclusions.

For the growing Christian, the path will be ever upward. Sometimes the road is steep. To me, at times, that road was almost sheer, even precipitous. But with all the prayers of the Bible in my notebooks, that beatific vision at the end of the Bible of all creation in worship before the Almighty—a perspective that reverberates in Revelation—kept me inching upward and forward to the higher realm that will someday climax a very long story.

As I conducted my investigation on prayer, I began to realize that the Bible pray-ers were like us, with similar problems and similar situations. "Elijah was a man with a nature like ours" (James 5:17). As a result, I have often prayed the prayers of the Bible, or have been prompted to a larger horizon by the prayers in this book.

My prayer for readers is that you will realize the love of God through the Bible prayers and will catch His desire that we come to Him, as needy people did throughout the biblical revelation.

Chapter One

GENESIS

KEY PRAYER VERSE FOR GENESIS

The key verse for Genesis is the same as the key verse for the entire Bible, Genesis 18:14, as mentioned in the introduction. How arresting that it is both a promise and a command! When Sarah questioned God's ability to give her a son, God responded:

> Is anything too hard for the LORD? At the appointed time I will return to you, about this time next year, and Sarah shall have a son.

Sarah had in mind her advanced age and lifelong sterility. The Lord first stated His ability to provide conception in her condition. In itself this verse is a *promise*. At the same time, although creation itself demonstrates a power beyond human comprehension, this is the first overt declaration in the Bible of God's omnipotence. The *command* is inherent in God's direction for the couple to believe in Him and to proceed according to His mandate.

KEY PRAYER THEMES FOR GENESIS

Several different prayer themes appear through Genesis. For convenience, two seem more prominent than others: (1) calling on the name of the Lord and (2) blessings and curses.

Calling on the Name of the Lord (4:26; 12:8; 13:4; 16:13; 21:33; 26:25)

Adam and Eve apparently "walked with God" and evidently carried on a conversation with Him. Their walking with God implied mutual communication with Him. Cain and Abel practiced a kind of prayer in their offerings (4:3-4). Apparently Abel had the one faithful heart (Hebrews 11:4). The first explicit mention of prayer comes with the grandson of Adam and Eve. Enosh was the son of Seth, the righteous replacement for Abel. "Seth" can mean "appointed" (to take Abel's place).

Seth named his son for one of the several Hebrew words preserved for the idea of "man." This word *enosh* attaches to itself an implication of weakness and dependency. It seems likely that Seth was aware of the awesome curse initiated by his parents' sin, and that he knew he was weak and needed God. His godly lineage culminated in Noah, who walked with God (6:9).

Since names in biblical times indicated character, Seth possibly either recognized his desperate need of God or "called" on God in the naming of his son: "To Seth also a son was born, and he called his name Enosh. At that time people began to call [*qara*] upon the name of the LORD" (4:26).

Calling may imply a sense of distance; even God called on Adam and Eve (the distance was in their minds, not God's). *Qara* can indicate a summons. When Adam hid from God, God *called* to him. Of course, God knew where Adam was, but it was necessary that Adam hear and respond to God's call. Sometimes the word *qara* can include the idea of loudness, implying that Enosh knew he was separated from God, so he "called" on Him. The idea of invocation comes into play here. How refreshing that God "calls" us and that we can "call" on Him! This call had an individual focus — Enosh calling on God.

In four other places, some editions translate *qara* by *worshipped* (12:8; 13:4; 21:33; 26:25). In three of these passages, Abraham's "call" to God is associated with his building an altar, and evidently the translators thought it would help our understanding to know that calling on God can be worshipping Him. An altar, then, would be a place of meeting with God.

Qara can also mean "to name something" (as "call" can in most European languages). Hagar responded to God's voice when she was fleeing her mistress, Sarah. He was sending her back to her mistress. (Many Christians associate her call to God with God's supplying a spring for Ishmael, but it actually occurred when God was redirecting her.) "So she called [*watiqraa* from *qara—called*] the name of the LORD who spoke to her, 'You are a God of seeing [*El Roi*]'" (16:13). (We can use the various names we will encounter in our prayers to God.) After Abraham made the covenant with Abimelech, he called on the name of the Lord (21:33). When the Lord appeared to Isaac in Beersheba, Isaac called on the name of the Lord (26:25).

Other Cases of Calling on the Lord

Psalm 116:2,13,17; 145:18; Acts 9:14; Romans 10:14; 2 Timothy 2:22; 1 Peter 1:17

Enosh's initiative was taken up repeatedly throughout the Bible. Samuel called for a sign (1 Samuel 12:17). At the great Baal contest, Elijah called on the name of the Lord (1 Kings 18:24). At the final restoration, all may call upon the Lord (Zephaniah 3:9).

Paul's well-known invitation is that "everyone who *calls* on the name of the Lord will be saved" (Romans 10:13, HCSB, emphasis added). His salutation to the Corinthian church includes all who call on the name of the Lord (1 Corinthians 1:2) and his instructions to Timothy joins Timothy to "those who call on the Lord from a pure heart" (2 Timothy 2:22). We can call on the Lord for our own benefit.

Christians today can freely call on the name of the Lord when in need, or when they fail to sense His presence, or in worship, or for all the various purposes in these biblical instances. The first mention of prayer in the Bible involves calling on God or His name.

Blessings and Curses (9:25-26; 14:19; 24:27; 27:27,29; 28:1,3-4; 32:26-29)

In the dawn of history God and His people blessed and they cursed. (This theme will not be prominent in later books of the Bible.) After creating Adam and Eve, God blessed them (1:28). Noah cursed Ham after his sin, and blessed Shem and Japheth (9:24-27). God's famous promise to bless those who bless Abram and curse those who curse him (12:3) is nearly a pledge of the way God will always act. He predictably has to honor those who honor Him and hold back blessings on His enemies (1 Samuel 2:30). Melchizedek's famous blessing on Abraham was primarily a blessing on God (14:18-20). When Isaac pronounced his blessing on Jacob, it included blessing and cursing (27:28-29). God blessed Jacob at Peniel (32:29). Many other blessings and curses abound throughout Genesis; their fundamental purpose was to further God's purposes for His people and to restrict the purposes of the wicked.

In later times, blessings and curses were often linked. Moses' instructions for the Israelites after they crossed the Jordan combined the two (Deuteronomy 27:12-26). Deborah included both in her great poem after their defeat of the northern Canaanites (Judges 5:23-24). Jesus' blessings (Matthew 5:3-11; Luke 6:20-22) as well as His woes (Matthew 23:13-35; Luke 6:24-26; and others) are an integral part of His message. Obviously, blessing occurs much more frequently in the New Testament (Luke 24:51,53; Romans 15:29; Ephesians 1:3; Revelation 5:12-13; and throughout) than cursing (Mark 11:21; Galatians 3:10,13; Hebrews 6:8). Only once do blessing and cursing occur together, and that is in James's warning that both should not come out of the same mouth (James 3:10).

The weight of evidence is that Christians should frequently bless God and one another, but should not curse. The book of Malachi will also major on blessings and curses in connection with the coming new Messenger of the covenant.

OTHER KINDS OF PRAYER

Another prayer concept introduced in Genesis that will become a major model for New Testament Christians (Romans 6:4; 8:4; Colossians 2:6; and many others) was the idea of "walking with God." When Enoch (also in the Seth line) walked with God, God translated him from earth to heaven so that he did not have to experience physical death (5:24). Walking with God implied a constant awareness of the presence of God; in the New Testament, it covered all a person's daily activities. Noah also walked with God (6:9). In establishing His covenant with Abraham, God commanded Abraham to "walk before Me" (17:1—the same word as used with Enoch and Noah).

Altars also appear frequently in Genesis (8:20, Noah; 22:9, Abraham; 33:20, Jacob), particularly in the earlier parts of the book. This indicates an awareness of the importance of offering something to God, not as a ritual but from the heart. It also indicates participating in a covenantal agreement. The first altar in the Bible also expressed gratitude (Noah in 8:20-21). This idea later became an important part of the Law, especially in Leviticus.

The prayer of Abraham's servant to find a wife for Isaac (24:12-14) demonstrates an important aspect of prayer: talking to God in the heart (24:45). This prayer tells us that God hears silent prayer. Hannah prayed silently for a child (1 Samuel 1:13). David confessed, "Even before a word is on my tongue, behold, O LORD, you know it altogether" (Psalm 139:4). "Isaac prayed to the LORD for his wife because she was barren" (25:21). The Lord responded, "The LORD granted his prayer" (25:21). Later Rachel prayed for a son and God "heard" (30:6). When Jacob prayed to be delivered from Esau (32:11-12) he appealed to God's previous promise to prosper him (26:24; 28:13-15), so it is legitimate to appeal to God on the basis of His promises.

The prayers in the rest of Genesis are well-known and have been instructive for Christians for centuries. Abraham pleaded for Sodom (18:23-32). God's listening to his pleas for the righteous through five repetitions — even though God knew there were not ten righteous in Sodom — tells us that it is all right to pray for something outside the immediate will of God if we are praying within the character of God. Abraham did not even pray for his family, but for the righteous. Abraham's frequent prayers are consequent of his title the "friend of God" (2 Chronicles 20:7; Isaiah 41:8; James 2:23).

God formally introduced Himself to Jacob in the dream at Bethel (28:10-22) in order to affirm to Jacob the promises He had made to Abraham, assuring Jacob of a wide inheritance. Jacob named the place "God's house" — "Bethel." Jacob vowed a pledge of fidelity to the Lord here, although he was still unbroken. He set up a stone as a marker for the place.

The Peniel incident (32:24-32) was preceded by a fervent prayer to be delivered from Esau (32:11-12). The wrestling indicated that with the supplanter Jacob, God's struggle with him changed him. Note that God Himself almost certainly initiated this encounter at Peniel. Jacob's fear of Esau would hardly have prompted him to tackle a stranger. God could have "set Jacob straight" early in the evening, but God knew that Jacob needed a struggle in order to "break" him to the point that he would cry out for a blessing. Jacob had stolen Esau's birthright and blessing and was now cowering at the thought of meeting Esau. The wisdom of the Lord required that it would take an all-night struggle to soften Jacob's stubbornness, and He even crippled Jacob in the process. Jacob would never be the same man.

Jacob's encounter at Peniel not only crippled him, but God blessed him there and changed his name. In blessing Joseph and his sons at the end of his life (48–49), Jacob praised,

The God before whom my fathers Abraham and Isaac walked,

    the God who has been my shepherd all my life long to this day,

    the angel who has redeemed me from all evil, bless the boys. (48:15-16)

Genesis reveals to us many kinds of prayers: calling on God, blessing and cursing, walking with God, crying out in an emergency, and appealing for mercy. Genesis significantly undertakes much teaching on prayer with a wide variety of communication with God. From this beginning, we see that prayer can befit any person in any situation in any place and condition.

EXODUS

KEY PRAYER VERSES FOR EXODUS

Exodus is a book of desperation in prayer. As Moses understood more and more the hopelessness of Israel without the constant intervention of God, he cried,

> If your presence will not go with me, do not bring us up from here. For how shall it be known that I have found favor in your sight, I and your people? Is it not in your going with us, so that we are distinct, I and your people, from every other people on the face of the earth? (33:15-16)

Nearly every Christian discovers the insight of this key prayer early in his or her pilgrimage. After coming to know Christ, we quickly meet with circumstances that convince us of our need for omnipotent intervention.

Moses remembered his prayer throughout the wilderness pilgrimage, but his people did not. It is astonishing that after the plagues and the crossing of the Red Sea, the Israelites could turn so quickly to a golden calf and to complaining about the food God miraculously provided for them. But do we not do the same thing today? When we are in need, we quickly sob out our plight, and then when God restores us to comfort, we resume ignoring the God we need supremely.

Have you ever prayed, "This time I didn't think about You, Lord. Just this once, come to my aid again, and I will serve You"?

Every Christian — every human — has found favor with God, although few continually identify it. Moses sensibly recognized that particular divine favor. Our favor may not be as spectacular as his, but practically every newly regenerated person recognizes God's favor, at least in his or her early stages. Knowing his need early, Moses instinctively asked for more. That God gave Moses this awareness is why we must ask for more.

Jesus further emphasized this concept. "For to everyone who has will more be given, and he will have an abundance. But from the one who has not, even what he has will be taken away" (Matthew 25:29). This relates to God's promise to bless those who bless Abraham; God will bless His own work. Moses prayed an important prayer that is not a cry: "Now therefore, if I have found favor in your sight, please show me now your ways, that I may know you in order to find favor in your sight" (33:13; see Matthew 25:29). Moses discerned that if God initiated favor, He would continue it. Jesus amplified this prayer in Luke 19:26: "I tell you that to everyone who has, more will be given." Once God initiates a favor on your behalf, you "have," so, like Moses, ask for more.

It would be easy to miss the significance of this important verse. We blame God quickly but seldom notice the divine intention in some benevolent work that God means as a blessing. How well we ignore God's voice, like Israel, and how quickly we forget the good God is pouring out on us. I memorized Exodus 33:16 many years ago, and asked God to open my eyes to the constant kindnesses He was sending me in order to facilitate either my growth or my work for Him.

KEY PRAYER THEME IN EXODUS
Crying Out to God (2:23; 3:7,9; 14:10; 15:25; 17:4; 22:23)
From their favored position under Joseph, the Israelites had passed into slavery, which became more onerous as time passed.

So they ruthlessly made the people of Israel work as slaves and made their lives bitter with hard service, in mortar and brick, and in all kinds of work in the field. In all their work they ruthlessly made them work as slaves. (1:13-14)

This cruelty led to the first cry to God in the Bible:

During those many days the king of Egypt died, and the people of Israel groaned because of their slavery and cried out for help. Their cry for rescue from slavery came up to God. And God heard their groaning, and God remembered his covenant with Abraham, with Isaac, and with Jacob. (2:23-24)

Their cry was the key that moved God to act on their behalf.

Then the LORD said, "I have surely seen the affliction of my people who are in Egypt and have heard their cry because of their taskmasters. I know their sufferings." (3:7; see also 3:9)

God's answer was to raise up a human deliverer who would be familiar with the lifestyle and attitudes within the Egyptian palace. Because Moses was frightened by God's call on Horeb, He reassured Moses, "I am the God of your father, the God of Abraham, the God of Isaac, the God of Jacob" (3:6). Generally, it was reassuring that God referred His people to their patriarchs; later He would refer them to King David. In his prayer about the golden calf, Moses referred God to the patriarchs (32:13; this prayer was surely painful to Moses). God always raises up exemplars to help us in our painful struggles.

Experienced Christians know that learning from suffering is an integral part of "walking with God." Joseph had procured for his nation an enviable status. At first, life was fresh with abundant favor in the new land. It took only the death of the favorable pharaoh to change their situation.

Yet is this not the path of every functioning Christian? With the first blush of joy and excitement at the new birth and regeneration, we hardly notice the harshness of the world until its incisive ridicule begins to pierce our armor (more of this in Ephesians 6). We instinctively look for God's intervention (the Israelites saw the plagues and the crossing of the Red Sea), but almost as quickly forget, as Israel did.

As long as we are in this life we will cry to God. As the Egyptians approached Israel beside the Red Sea, the Hebrews "cried out to the LORD" for help (14:10). The Lord sweetened the bitter waters of Marah when Moses cried to Him (15:25). He brought water from the rock at Meribah when again Moses "cried to the LORD" (17:4). These cries were always uttered in times of extreme need. The Lord hears the cry of His people. He promised the Israelites, "You shall not mistreat any widow or fatherless child. If you do mistreat them, and they cry out to me, I will surely hear their cry" (22:22-23).

God's intervention in our lives elicits praise. After crossing the sea, Moses and his people sang a magnificent paean to the Lord (this time a joyful cry; 15:1-19). Then Miriam led the women in singing with tambourines and dancing (15:20-21). You may object, "But I have never crossed a sea or a river on dry land." As I have worked these decades with the Bible prayers, I have grown to realize how often I am oblivious to a truly divine work of God in my life. We may be surprised in eternity at how obvious God's work should have been.

Note that the poetry of deliverance (15:1-18) is not thanksgiving; it is praise. We will see more of thanksgiving later. The mighty power of God overwhelmed the Egyptians as well as the Israelites. They had seen the divine energy do enormous miracles for them in the plagues but had failed to praise it. The Israelites required the gigantic holding of the waters and the drowning of the Egyptian army to move them to appropriate praise. Later in the poem Jethro blessed the Lord for the deliverance (18:10-11). Are we as reluctant, or blind, as they?

In his prayer about the golden calf, Moses asked God to blot out his own name if He did not forgive the iniquity of His people. This says much about sincerity in prayer. When Moses asked to see God's glory, forbidden to humans, God allowed a partial glimpse of his "back"—again, an indication of the power of earnestness in prayer. After God replaced the two broken tablets, "Moses quickly bowed his head toward the earth and worshiped" (34:8). Note the double care of Moses—first, for the glory of God, and second, for the deliverance of His nation. Moses' whole being, body and mind, was constantly in a state of crying to the Lord.

At Meribah, Moses did not specify the remedy for Israel's thirst. He cried to the Lord for advice. In warning Israel about their treatment of the widows and orphans, God Himself spoke of their cry as a prayer (22:22-23). Evidently, those cries touched God's heart. Moses' union with God made his face shine.

Something remotely like this happened to me once. After a particularly deep season of prayer, I had to leave my solitary place and meet some friends. The first woman who saw me exclaimed, "What has happened to you? Your face is aglow." Of course she was not seeing visible light from my countenance, but it made me cry to the Lord, "Father, may my countenance turn the hearts of many to you."

The fitting nature of the prayers throughout Genesis show what we should learn early: that God is our source. But a young nation and young Christians find themselves early in the quandary of suffering, and we need to learn God's response to our cries. The cries of Exodus sound sometimes painful, sometimes plaintive, sometimes joyful, and, above all, they capture the heart of God. We will study more about sincerity later, but already we have arrived on the threshold of knowing how to touch the great heart of a caring God.

Chapter Three

LEVITICUS, NUMBERS, DEUTERONOMY

KEY PRAYER VERSE FOR LEVITICUS

While most Bible dictionaries treat sacrifice and offering under the single heading "Sacrifice," it is convenient for our understanding to distinguish between them. Sacrifice carries away our *demerit*. In offering, we are giving something; it carries heavenward our *merit*.[1] Significantly, this Bible book on offering spells out the specifics most clearly while the nation was still in the wilderness, before they entered the Promised Land.

Although many offerings prescribed are thank offerings, the various sacrifices served mainly for atonement rather than gratitude. Note the key verse, repeated over and over:

> And the priest shall make atonement for them, and they shall be forgiven. (4:20)

Although God does not have body parts, the Bible can only inform us about Him in terms of the world we live in, that is, in an anthropomorphic sense. The phrase "pleasing aroma," which occurs in Genesis, Exodus, Leviticus, Numbers, Ezra, and Ezekiel, is a biblical expression that indicates the enormity of the pleasure God takes in our offerings. In the New Testament, we are called the "aroma of Christ" to the Father (2 Corinthians 2:15) and to Paul, the gift of the Philippians was a "fragrant offering, a sacrifice acceptable and pleasing to God" (Philippians 4:18).

KEY PRAYER THEME FOR LEVITICUS
Offering and Sacrifice

Every chapter in Leviticus is directly or indirectly concerned with offering and sacrifice, the key theme for the book. Most Bible readers dread plowing through the elaborate instructions for the various kinds of offerings, but these instructions point to some important aspects of prayer that most Christians ignore.

God wanted the Israelites — and us — to present their offerings, not as a thankful return for favors but for two main reasons. Primarily, we are to appreciate God in Himself, not for what He does for us. In Israel's case, the elaborate offerings preceded the occupation of the Holy Land, which would have later inspired thanksgiving. Israel had much already to be thankful for — the plagues, the manna, the provision of safety, preservation, and drink. Strikingly, many people built altars with thanksgiving as a motive *before* God gave the instructions for the tabernacle (Abraham built four altars; Noah's altar of thanksgiving is perhaps the most famous). God's nation was to learn to elevate their God, even at cost. Christians today may not build an altar as Noah did, but we can present all kinds of material offerings and actions that are a pleasing offering to God.

Secondly, the Levitical offering often atones through sacrifice, which, of course, finds its fulfillment in the enormous offering of Golgotha. One aspect missing from our present-day offering (in services) that the Israelites practiced is corporate offering (4:13-21; closely tied to corporate confession, which we will see later with Ezra and Nehemiah). Theologians have led us to appreciate the enormity of the sacrifice on the cross by pointing to the many meanings in the atonement offerings.

The sacrifices to pagan gods were literal food and drink. This physical sense is somewhat foreign to the Levitical system, where the offerings indicated spiritual exercises. God does not need to be fed by human hands; what pleases Him is the "sweet-smelling savor" that we are in Christ. If fully and appropriately carried out, the sacrificial system of the Pentateuch should have made the people aware of the dangers of sin because of the frequency of repetition.

The meat offerings were either eaten by the offerer or by the priest (not by God), or else they were burned. The drink offerings were not drunk; they were poured out, as the blood was poured out. None of the unbloody sacrifices were made in isolation; they had to be offered in conjunction with a bloody offering ("the life of the flesh is in the blood"; 17:11). This should have indicated deep spiritual truths to those making the offering or sacrifice. The many kinds of offerings are carefully detailed in practically all Bible dictionaries and encyclopedias, and are beyond the scope of this writing. Their importance is seen in the fact that Leviticus mentions offerings and sacrifices 274 times.

The offerings in the Old Testament prepared the way for more spiritual offerings in the New Testament. Even David anticipated this deeper significance: "You do not want a sacrifice, or I would give it. . . . The sacrifice pleasing to God is a broken spirit" (Psalm 51:16-17, HCSB). Rather than a physical sacrifice, offerings in the New Testament were of a spiritual nature, involving the heart (Matthew 9:13; Mark 12:33; and many more). See especially 2 Corinthians 8:12 (where service is acceptable according to the eagerness of the server) and 2 Timothy 4:6 (Paul's life was poured out as a drink offering). Even the offerer's body was a *living* sacrifice (Romans 12:1). This concept is later applied to our praying without ceasing.

The priests making the offerings had to be purified in elaborate ceremonies (chapters 8–10). We New Testament Christians are a "royal priesthood" (1 Peter 2:9) so our prayer offerings (among other kinds of offerings) must also be of the highest sanctity we can offer to God. Old Testament priests were special persons; New Testament priests should be thoroughly separated from the world.

Intercession in History

While Leviticus and Exodus are more important theologically because of their prefiguring of Calvary, Numbers takes the ascendancy in prayer because of its importance in intercession, a major aspect of this historical book.

KEY PRAYER VERSE FOR NUMBERS

The key prayer verse for Numbers occurs as an injunction for Israel not to fear "the giants" in the land of Canaan. It happens after the ten spies brought their dismal report. Joshua admonished the nation,

> Only do not rebel against the LORD. And do not fear the people of the land, for they are bread for us. Their protection is removed from them, and the LORD is with us; do not fear them. (14:9)

In announcing the removal of protection from the Canaanites, Joshua was reminding Israel of the obvious protection they had had since the beginning of the plagues. We New Testament followers have the assurance of the continual presence of Christ with us (Matthew 28:20).

KEY PRAYER THEME FOR NUMBERS
Intercession (12:13; 14:13-21; 21:7)

The key prayer theme dominating the important narrative sections centers on interceding. All the intercession in this book shows a leader interceding for his people. How interesting that prayers in Numbers requesting something follow sequentially the prayers in Leviticus that give God the glory due to His name through offering!

After the Israelites compounded their sins by rejecting the good advice of Joshua and Caleb, Moses prayed one of the most powerful intercessions in the Bible. The Pentateuch records twelve intercessory prayers by this great man of God. Another key verse sums up what most of them were about: "Please pardon the iniquity of this people, according to the greatness of your steadfast love, just as you have forgiven this people, from Egypt until now" (14:19).

The sincerity of these remarkable prayers evidences the fact that after the incident of the golden calf, Moses even prayed that if God would not forgive the people, He should take Moses' life instead.

The first recorded "prayer" of Numbers resembles the "prayer" of fasting. In Numbers 6, God gave Moses the instructions for the Nazirite vow. This private covenant prepares a way for a man or woman wishing to set aside a period of his or her life for complete devotion to God. Certain food and drink were not to be consumed and the individual was not to cut his or her hair during the time of the commitment. This special vow must have pleased the Lord. He stated, "He is holy to the LORD during the time of consecration" (6:8, HCSB).

The first five chapters of Numbers are mainly concerned with various duties of the Levites and priests (continuing the tutoring on offering in Leviticus and preparing the way for intercession). After the Nazirite instruction, God gave the thrilling priestly blessing that Aaron and the priests should speak over the people:

The Lord bless you and keep you;

the Lord make his face to shine upon you and be gracious to you;

the Lord lift up his countenance upon you and give you peace.

(6:24-26)

Moses became a consummate intercessor for his people, usually valuing them above himself. After the fire of the Lord broke out at Taberah, "the people cried out to Moses and Moses prayed to the Lord, and the fire died down" (11:2). When Moses complained to the Lord about his heavy load, God answered his prayer by granting seventy elders to assist him in the onerous burden (11:10-17).

After God dealt with Aaron and Miriam for their rebellion against Moses, Moses interceded for the skin disease God inflicted on Miriam: "And Moses cried to the Lord, 'O God, please heal her— please'" (12:13). Miriam experienced a delay of the answer for a full week outside the camp. In the Bible God does not always answer prayer immediately. Throughout Scripture, God demonstrates His wisdom when He delays an answer. Miriam needed to learn a lesson.

Although no prayer is recorded in the rebellion of Korah, Moses dealt with the instructions he received from God, both with Korah and later with the people angry about Korah's death. He made it clear that his instructions were directly from God (16:4,46). In this case, God did all the talking. We have the same phenomenon (God doing most of the talking) on one of the occasions when Moses brought water from the rock (20:7).

The Lord once again threatened the destruction of Israel after they refused the report of the spies sent into the Promised Land. Moses repeatedly, in many of his prayers, referred to the character of God (see 14:17 on the strength of the Lord). Once again that great intercessor had to plead for his people:

"The Lord is slow to anger and abounding in steadfast love, forgiving iniquity and transgression, but he will by no means clear the guilty, visiting the iniquity of the fathers on the children, to the third and the fourth generation." Please pardon the iniquity of this people, according to the greatness of your steadfast love, just as you have forgiven this people, from Egypt until now. (14:18-19)

A significant prayer request in the Bible occurs in the incident of the snakes, when the Israelites begged Moses to intercede for them:

And the people came to Moses and said, "We have sinned, for we have spoken against the LORD and against you. [Remember the principle that God blesses those who bless His work and curses those who curse His work.] Pray to the LORD, that he take away the serpents from us." So Moses prayed for the people. (21:7)

The ending of the book concerns divisions within the Promised Land and with some instructions on inheritance. But the key to the nation's arrival across from Jericho lies clearly in the skillful and godly intercession of their leader, who never gave up and never stopped praying for a rebellious people.

Intercession characterized the rest of the Bible repeatedly. Jesus informed the disciples at the foot of the Mount of Transfiguration that the demon in the possessed boy could come out only by prayer (Mark 9:29; some manuscripts add fasting). Jesus interceded for Peter (Luke 22:32) and, on the cross, for forgiveness for His persecutors (Luke 23:34).

KEY PRAYER VERSE FOR DEUTERONOMY

Significantly, the key verse for this "Second Law," mainly a recapitulation of all that has preceded in the Pentateuch, forms a fitting climax to the preceding instructions for prayer:

And you shall rejoice before the LORD your God, you and your sons and your daughters, your male servants and your female servants, and the Levite that is within your towns, since he has no portion or inheritance with you. (12:12)

After His people learned to call on the Lord, bless Him, cry to Him, and offer to Him, God granted to His people the high privilege of holy joy.

KEY PRAYER THEMES FOR DEUTERONOMY
"No" Answers to Prayer

Early in the book, Moses offered a surprise to pray-ers: an "unanswered" prayer, that is, an answer of "no." He retold the story of his prayer to enter the Holy Land (which God had forbidden when he struck the rock; 3:25-27). We have already seen God's refusal to end Moses' life when he prayed to die. That same "answer"—a "no" answer to a prayer to die—was given to Elijah (1 Kings 19:4), Job (Job 3:3), Jeremiah (Jeremiah 20:14), and Jonah (Jonah 4:3).

"No" answers to our prayers have puzzled Christians for centuries. Significantly, the Bible gives many examples of "no" answers to show us that God is listening. I have become convinced by my own "unanswered" prayers that God's wisdom far exceeds ours and that He probably is grieved when we blame Him for His good judgment that far exceeds ours. When I prayed for healing from my cellulitis, the answer was to allow my bloodstream to become infected and prolong my weeks in the hospital. I affirmed God's wisdom in this on that hospital bed, and the Lord brought a flood of new insights, plus an understanding that I was to travel less and write more!

Another "unanswered" prayer happened when the Israelites' demand for meat resulted in the quail that killed many of them (Numbers 11:33). After the Israelites' attempt to placate God in their rejection of the spies' advice, God allowed the consequences to play out: they could not enter Canaan at that time (Numbers 14:22-23). After Saul's rejection, God did not answer him (1 Samuel 28:6), another example of many "no" answers in the Bible. Saul's lust for power had caused him to exhaust his opportunities. The abominations of Judah turned God from their prayers (Jeremiah 11:14, 14:11-12; Ezekiel 8:18; 14:3). God's answer to David for David's baby son was "no" (2 Samuel 12:16-20). Sin or surrounding circumstances often produce a sovereign "no" from God. All God's answers demonstrate His wisdom.

Jesus denied the Pharisees' request for a sign (Matthew 16:4), and He also corrected the request that James and John sit at His right hand (Matthew 20:20-23). Jesus sometimes denied the request of those He healed to accompany Him (that is, Jesus; Mark 5:17-19). Jesus always remained discerning about His followers. The leaders' requests to die came from a desire for relief or from a wrong motive. Some of the "no" answers (like King Saul's) were in response to wickedness (Isaiah 59:2). When Jesus denied a request, it was sometimes to avoid exposing His Messiahship or because of His divine wisdom (as in the request for James and John to sit at Jesus' right hand).

Moses' forty-day fasts were either in sorrow (9:8-20,25-29) or in such earnestness that he placed his requests on a more urgent level than food (10:10-11). One of the main characteristics of his prayers is passionate involvement in God's causes.

Rejoicing (12:7,12,18; 14:26; 16:11; 26:11; 27:7)

A second major theme in Deuteronomy commands the offerers to rejoice. In the first injunction to rejoice, God commanded the Israelites to celebrate at the place (tabernacle and temple) He chose: "And there you shall eat before the LORD your God, and you shall rejoice, you and your households, in all that you undertake, in which the LORD your God has blessed you" (12:7).

Later, in connection with various offerings, God commanded, "Rejoice before the LORD your God in all that you undertake" (12:18). Still later, for those unable to bring the prescribed sacrifices, God allowed a tithe of money with the injunction: "Spend the money for whatever you desire—oxen or sheep or wine or strong drink, whatever your appetite craves. And you shall eat there before the LORD your God and rejoice, you and your household" (14:26).

The festivals abound with joy. In the Feast of Weeks, God made joy a major part of the celebration:

> And you shall rejoice before the LORD your God, you and your son
> and your daughter, your male servant and your female servant, the
> Levite who is within your towns, the sojourner, the fatherless, and
> the widow who are among you, at the place that the LORD your God
> will choose, to make his name dwell there. (16:11)

In connection with the Firstfruits, God told His people, after they presented their offerings: "And you shall rejoice in all the good that the LORD your God has given to you and to your house, you, and the Levite, and the sojourner who is among you" (26:11).

The order of the prayers in the Pentateuch encapsulates the general order of the development of prayer for all time. It begins with calling on God, blessing and cursing according to the divine character and work, crying to God in desperation, offering to God, interceding for our fellows, but, significantly, ends with the command to rejoice. The writer tells us at the end of the book, "And there has not arisen a prophet since in Israel like Moses, whom the LORD knew face to face" (34:10). Rejoicing also characterizes the last book in the Bible.

Chapter Four

JOSHUA, JUDGES, RUTH

KEY PRAYER VERSE FOR JOSHUA

In Joshua, God fulfills a series of promises He had made long before, beginning with Abraham. At the end of the conquest, the writer boasts about the faithfulness of God. This is not only a key prayer verse for Joshua, but also serves well for the whole Bible.

> Not one word of all the good promises that the LORD had made to the house of Israel had failed; all came to pass. (21:45)

Even when men failed (Aaron, Miriam, and many others), God's Word reflects His unvarying nature. Joshua 21:44 tells us, "And the LORD gave them rest on every side just as he had sworn to their fathers."

One aspect of the divine promises implies the permanency of God's integrity: "I have set my bow in the cloud, and it shall be a sign of the covenant between me and the earth" (Genesis 9:13). Over the years the covenants and promises of God have filled many books.

KEY PRAYER THEME FOR JOSHUA
God Fulfilling His Promises (6:2,20; 8:1,24; 21:45)

Joshua, like Genesis, contains a number of beginnings. In this case God led Israel to occupy the Promised Land. The key prayer theme points to God fulfilling His promises. Joshua also contains several endings — God fulfilling age-old promises about occupying Canaan. Also like Genesis, Joshua has a number of different kinds of prayers.

In the first prayer in this book, Joshua gave an oath when the spies told Rahab that if she kept her promise of not betraying them, she and her family would be spared (2:14-20). We shall encounter many oaths as we proceed through the Bible. Oaths are usually primarily to God (ultimately even this one), and swearing an oath is a matter of great solemnity. The spies were swearing to Rahab about God's ultimate intention for His people. Most later oaths in the Old Testament are directed to God.

Later, with the New Covenant, Jesus warned sternly that we should not swear in any way (Matthew 5:33-37); our word should be sufficient to establish the validity of what we say. In Matthew 12:34-37, Jesus warned about the effectiveness of our words and cautioned that for safety they should be few.

Oaths and Vows

An oath verifies that a statement is true or a vow will be kept. Jesus answered Caiaphas under oath and Paul made three oaths. A vow was usually an expression of devotion. Some vows attached conditions. The Nazirite vow did not.

Prayer enters in Joshua 5, when the forty years of wandering are explained by the fact that Israel did not listen to God's instructions (5:6). The Bible often refers to God speaking to humans instead of people speaking to God. This too may be considered a kind of prayer. Prayer may be the human talking to God, God talking to the human, or, in some cases (with Moses especially), a dialogue.

A dialogue occurs in Joshua 5:13-15. God met Joshua in much the same way He spoke to Moses. God began preparing Joshua for the role he would play in the conquest of Jericho. This moment was holy, for God commanded Joshua to remove the sandals from his feet, as He had ordered Moses. God gave Joshua special and exceptional directions about entering Jericho.

As mentioned, the key prayer theme for this book centers on God making and keeping promises, a kind of instruction that would be useful to Israel for centuries as encouragement to believe God. By using this particular technique (promising the fall of the walls of Jericho), only God could get credit for the taking of the city (6:2-5). God fulfilled this promise in 6:20.

After such a victory, one member of the nation became overconfident and surreptitiously took some of the loot that should have been "set apart" (consecrated to God), and Israel was defeated. After this incident in Ai, Joshua "tore his clothes and fell to the earth on his face before the ark of the LORD until the evening" (7:6), an early instance of humility that becomes so vital in the New Testament. Achan and his family were executed. God had admonished Israel in 5:6; now He showed how serious He was about His work and the holiness that should accompany it. Once again He promised that, with His instructions and help, the nation would conquer Ai (8:18). God kept His promise (8:24).

Joshua built an altar after the defeat of Ai, following the precedent with Noah, Abraham, and Isaac. Altars occurred mainly in the earlier parts of the Old Testament and were usually a testament of gratitude to God, serving for sacrifice or offering. Later, in the temple, altars would point to the sacrificial spirit important in prayer. In these earlier days, altars were mainly between an individual and God; ultimately, they would serve divine purposes for the nation.

Because altars were for God, a major dispute arose between the eastern and western tribes when the former built an altar. Peace was restored only after the eastern tribes reassured Joshua that their altar was symbolic and not for burnt offering and sacrifice.

A major concomitant of prayer appears in 9:3-27: the frightening consequences of proceeding without prayer. The failure to pray demonstrates graphically the consequences of failing to consult God, such as when the nation failed to consult God about the pretense of the Gibeonites. We can sympathize with the Gibeonites, in view of the other conquests Israel was making, but God had told the Israelites to have no communion with any of the Canaanite peoples. The Israelite oath to spare the Gibeonites shows how foolish an oath can be (Jesus later warned sternly about oaths — Matthew 5:33-37).

Probably the most famous prayer in Joshua is his commanding the sun to stand still while Israel defeated the Amorites (10:12-14). This prayer offered unmistakable, dramatic proof of the validity of the edicts to enter the Promised Land. The specific prayer of Joshua reassured him and Israel that God would also fulfill general prayers.

After the defeat of much of Canaan, Joshua instituted another kind of prayer. Since the whole congregation assembled at the tent of meeting (where God manifested Himself), we may regard the following divisions by lots as a result of prayer (chapters 18 and 19). This strange kind of "prayer" was peculiar to and appropriate for the circumstances of dividing unknown land among twelve tribes.

A similar mystery had been presented in Exodus 28:15-30, where the Urim and Thummim were placed on Aaron's heart when he went before the Lord. From the time of Moses, the high priest determined the will of God by the Urim and Thummim, but we know little about them. These kinds of prayer disappear early in the history of the nation and are outside the teaching in the New Testament. In the later development of prayer, amulets, symbolic or literal, disappear.

Prayer must not become a form of superstition nor must prayer try to manipulate God. Jesus made this specific in His instruction on prayer in Matthew 6:5-15.

The climax of Joshua comes in 21:45, the key verse for this book, where the writer rejoiced in God's faithfulness to His people. The story started many years before when God promised this land to Abraham. Now Israel occupied it. Israel had a long history of patience and divine miracles that brought them into the land. God had kept His word.

Our specific prayers respond to God's revelation. Specific prayers narrow the field and move our general prayers to specific ones. God had a powerful purpose in causing the sun to stand still.

KEY PRAYER VERSE FOR JUDGES

Deborah's song fits appropriately all the work of the various judges to come; it attributes all success to God. After she defeated the Canaanites, her poem includes the key verse of this section:

> Hear, O kings; give ear, O princes;
>> to the LORD I will sing;
>> I will make melody to the LORD, the God of Israel. (5:3)

The poem of Deborah (and possibly Barak) is one of the most exquisite poems in all literature. In it Deborah related the various stages of the victory. Beauty of language may well characterize successful prayer.

KEY PRAYER THEME FOR JUDGES

Prayer for Deliverance in Crisis (3:9; 4:3; 5:1-31; 6:15,36-37)

Most of today's Christians remain as confused about the many cycles of sin and restoration in Judges as the Israelites themselves were.

Without a current leader or dynasty to constantly redirect them to the Lord, "everyone did what was right in his own eyes" (17:6). In each of their various apostasies, God compassionately raised up a leader who would restore their focus.

The raising up of the various judges specifically answered the several prayers of Moses and probably Joshua. Our prayers continue to be effective after we utter them. Moses' prayers continued their effective work long after he ascended Mount Nebo. Deliverance from crisis corresponded to the general prayer theme of Judges. The prayers of the earlier leaders (for example, Abraham and Jacob) built on God's promises made centuries before and appropriated by Moses and Joshua.

The opening verse of the book sets the tone for the ever-repeated cry: "After the death of Joshua, the people of Israel inquired of the LORD, 'Who shall go up first for us against the Canaanites, to fight against them?'" (1:1). They would repeat that cry over and over. After the first test of surrounding them with wicked enemies, the people turned to Baal and the Ashtaroths. When the nation failed their first encounter with hostile forces, God handed them over to the king of Aram and the Israelites "cried out to the LORD" (3:9), as they did again a few verses later (3:15). After the overwhelming defeat of the Canaanite Sisera, Deborah (and Barak?) wrote the glorious song of 5:2-31, a song that was a token of God's patience and kindness through repeated apostasies.

The Gideon story begins in Judges 6. In his call to Gideon, the Lord astonishingly called him a "mighty warrior" (HCSB). Gideon certainly reacted with cowardice, even demanding a sign (the fleece), so this call and work of God shows what God intends to do with weakness: turn a coward into a mighty warrior. The Bible overflows with God's calling and working through the weak and lowly. After Gideon heard a man's dream about the barley bread destroying a Midianite, "he worshiped" (7:15) and went on to conquer the enemy (as a mighty warrior).

The nation called Jephthah after the people turned again to the Baals and Ashtaroths. This new judge arose when God "became impatient over the misery of Israel" (10:16). Because the national leaders had previously rejected him, when they came to him for help, he made his own terms. "And Jephthah spoke all his words before the LORD at Mizpah" (11:11). His foolish vow teaches us that God takes vows seriously. An oath is more akin to swearing, while a vow is a pledge. Jephthah kept his vow, an early symbol of Jesus' cautioning against oaths.

Samson became a judge after the Lord had to reassure his parents, Manoah and his wife, through an astonishing theophany (an appearance of God to a human). Manoah's prayer (13:15-19) shows how prayer at times becomes back-and-forth in order to make obedience clear. God clarified the steps of obedience in Judges 17–19 for His glory.

Later, when Samson became thirsty, he petitioned the Lord for water and the Lord provided it. Samson's last prayer was a prayer for revenge because the Philistines had gouged out his eyes, and in his death he killed more Philistines than he had in life. This was already God's will; Samson finally obeyed and asked for what God had required.

With the sordid story of the killing of the Levite's wife, God did not raise up a judge, but the men of Israel once again fasted and inquired of the Lord, and the Lord gave a powerful victory to Israel over Benjamin (the Levite lived in Benjamin). The other tribes had sworn that no man would permit his daughter to marry a Benjamite. God ultimately provided them with a way to furnish wives to the Benjamites by subterfuge. The other tribes advised the Benjamites to snatch a wife from the women participating in a dance in feasting (21:16-23).

KEY PRAYER VERSE FOR RUTH

As Boaz recognized the sterling character of Ruth, he prayed,

> The LORD repay you for what you have done, and a full reward be
> given you by the LORD, the God of Israel, under whose wings you
> have come to take refuge! (2:12)

The answer to Boaz's prayer echoed down through the centuries
through a dynasty that produced the Messiah's lineage. Boaz, like us,
did not envision the ultimate outcome of his prayer. God often uses
prayer for multiple purposes. We do not need to understand God in
order to obey Him.

KEY PRAYER THEME FOR RUTH

Speaking a Blessing (1:8-9; 2:4,12,19-20; 3:10; 4:14)

Blessings saturate the book of Ruth, blessings appropriate for her
character and for the founding of the royal family. Naomi first pro-
nounced a benediction as she blessed her daughters-in-law (1:8-9).
Twice in 2:19-20, Naomi blessed Boaz for his notice of Ruth. After
Boaz bought the property of the two former husbands and declared
Ruth to be his wife,

> All the people who were at the gate and the elders said, "We are wit-
> nesses. May the LORD make the woman, who is coming into your
> house, like Rachel and Leah, who together built up the house of
> Israel. May you act worthily in Ephrathah and be renowned in
> Bethlehem, and may your house be like the house of Perez, whom
> Tamar bore to Judah, because of the offspring that the LORD will
> give you by this young woman." (4:11-12)

Notice that a Gentile was chosen by God to be a blessing and to be blessed. Remember Rahab. The blessings of Ruth would extend for generations to come.

The progression of people learning to pray in the Pentateuch instructs us well. The promises to Moses and Joshua prepared the historical "blessings" in Ruth. Joshua, Judges, and Ruth illustrate the fact that God uses our limited understanding of prayer in infinite ways, beyond the purposes of our immediate life span.

Chapter Five

SAMUEL, KINGS, CHRONICLES

KEY PRAYER VERSE FOR 1 SAMUEL

Samuel showed unusual insight into prayer when, after the people foolishly forced him to anoint Saul as king, he told them,

> As for me, I vow that I will not sin against the LORD by ceasing to pray for you. (12:23, HCSB)

Israel had failed to pray about accepting the Gibeonites (Joshua 9:14) and later God chastised Israel for not praying (Zephaniah 1:6). *The sin of prayerlessness is perhaps the greatest sin we can commit in reference to prayer.*

Saul's reign precipitated one of the most puzzling episodes in the Bible. Samuel probably foresaw the dire conditions under the many wicked kings ahead. Surely his prayer foresaw the future of the nation. When sin seems to be in control, we sin when we do not turn to God as prayerfully as we can.

Side issues. God "hears" our thoughts. We have already seen that Hannah prayed silently for a son. When Abraham's servant was seeking a wife for Isaac, the servant prayed silently (Genesis 24:45). Nehemiah prayed silently before Artaxerxes when the prophet was about to request permission to go to Jerusalem (Nehemiah 2:4). In all three of these cases, God answered the prayer, although each was not verbalized audibly.

After God answered Hannah's petition, her prayer of praise (2:1-10) was aloud and was concerned mainly with her own reversal of circumstances, which she applied to all the needy and righteous. One possibility of meaning for the name "Samuel" is that it is a wordplay for "requested of God." Hannah's insight into the ways of God, bringing greatness out of smallness (reversal of circumstances), shows unusual perception into God's nature, which is later expanded in Mary's glorious Magnificat (Luke 1:51-53) and highlighted by Jesus (in the Matthew 5:3-12 and Luke 6:20-23 versions of the Sermon on the Mount and Sermon on the Plain).

Hannah's prayer begins with the acknowledgement that "there is none holy like the LORD" (2:2). Her prayer glorifies God rather than God's gift. This prayer also significantly uses the word *anointed* for the first time (2:10; note that this occurred before Israel had a king).

God judged the two sons of Eli, Hophni and Phinehas, because they "treated the offering of the LORD with contempt" (2:17). God once again reiterated His principle of blessing those who bless Him or His representative and cursing those who set themselves against Him: "Those who honor me I will honor, and those who despise me shall be lightly esteemed" (2:30).

God had told Abraham that He would bless those who blessed Abraham and curse those who cursed him (Genesis 12:3), and here it becomes a principle for all God's people through the centuries. To accomplish His purposes through His creation, God must bless those who are doing His work and negate the work of those opposing Him.

Samuel's call from the Lord in 3:9-15 illustrates prayer as dialogue. It also shows God's confidence in a little boy. Instead of speaking directly to the priest, Eli (to whom God ascribed the wickedness of his sons), God chose to speak to a child. Beginning here and continuing throughout Samuel's ministry, God chose this little boy to hear His voice.

An example of superstition in prayer surfaces as the Israelites use the presence of the ark to ensure their victory over the Philistines (4:3); God intended for the ark to remain with His chosen people. This battle took the lives of Eli's wicked sons. After the Philistines captured and possessed the ark for some twenty years, Samuel volunteered to pray for the nation in mourning (7:5), and the Israelites confessed their sins with fasting (7:6). After the consequent Israelite victory, Samuel set up a memorial stone and called it "Ebenezer" ("Stone of Help" — 7:12).

KEY PRAYER THEME FOR 1 SAMUEL
Inquiring of the Lord (9:9; 10:22; 22:10; 23:2,4; 28:6; 30:7-8)

Israel's demand for a king seems reasonable in view of the wickedness of Samuel's sons Joel and Abijah. However, omnisciently aware of Solomon and his successors, God cautioned Moses that a king should not "acquire many horses for himself" (Deuteronomy 17:16). God also warned, "He shall not acquire many wives for himself, lest his heart turn away" (17:17): an early warning that authority perverts. God's discourse to Moses outlined what He expected from a sovereign. God's word to Moses later proved accurate in both the southern and northern kingdoms. The various histories of the dynasties in the north and of David's dynasty in the south bear out God's word, and even prove that God can use adverse circumstances to accomplish His will (Romans 8:28). God's baffling choice of Saul demonstrates the certainty of His word to Moses.

Inquiry could be made through a priest or prophet (a "seer"), through the Urim and Thummim if the high priest was available, through direct inquiry by someone to the Lord, or through dreams (28:6). The Bible sometimes tells us the method of inquiry, but not often. Saul was the first to inquire directly to the Lord, through Samuel (9:9-20). The people themselves inquired of the Lord about finding God's choice (10:22). Later, after Samuel remonstrated with the people for their determination to have a king, Samuel called on the Lord, who sent thunder and rain to validate Samuel's words (12:16-18).

Saul, jealous for his position, made his troops take a rash oath that required fasting. Only the loyalty of the people saved Jonathan's life. David repeatedly inquired of the Lord; many subsequent facts about David indicate that he leaned on the Lord for guidance. In the long saga of Saul against David, Ahimelech, son of a priest (possibly a high priest) inquired of the Lord for David (22:10). In the war with the Philistines, David two times inquired of the Lord (23:2,4) and twice about Saul (if Keilah and his men would surrender David into Saul's hand—23:11-12). Near the end of 1 Samuel, David again inquired of the Lord when he was surrounded by Amalekites (30:7-8).

When Saul inquired of the Lord and the Lord did not answer, Saul tragically inquired of the witch of Endor (28:7-19). This incident reveals what Moses and Samuel had foreseen about a king for Israel. Saul's lust for power led him to wrong supernatural ends (Leviticus 19:31).

The theme of inquiring of the Lord continued throughout the Bible. In 1 Kings 22:8, Jehoshaphat forced Ahab to inquire of the Lord by the prophet Micaiah. Later Josiah inquired of the Lord by the prophetess Huldah (2 Kings 22:18).

Modern men and women of God should still seek His guidance. We do not have the methods available to Old Testament figures; we have the far better Counselor promised by Jesus (John 15:26). He may speak to us through an inner witness from the Holy Spirit, through the ministry of gifted Christians, or even through dreams. God wants to guide His people. Responsibility prays for the guidance of the Holy Spirit!

KEY PRAYER VERSE FOR 2 SAMUEL

After David's victory over the Philistines and the death of Saul, David wrote a psalm of triumph. The key prayer verse for this book reflects David's lifelong dependence on God:

> I call upon the LORD, who is worthy to be praised,
>> and I am saved from my enemies. (22:4)

We have seen how people began to call on the Lord after Enosh, and continued to do so throughout biblical history.

KEY PRAYER THEME FOR 2 SAMUEL

Celebration of Victories Through God (6:5,14-18,20-23; 22:1-4)

Early in the book, David continued his habit of inquiring of the Lord. He asked where he should go to be anointed king of Judah; the Lord sent him to Hebron (2:1). Later (2:5), David blessed the men of Jabesh-gilead for burying Saul. In chapter 3, we have the rare example of David uttering a curse on Joab for murdering Abner (3:29); David later fasted over Abner's death. After being anointed king of all Israel, he once again inquired of the Lord if he should go against the Philistines. With God's "yes" answer David even inquired about the method of battle and God used a supernatural direction for the defeat of his enemies (5:22-23).

Uzzah died when he touched the ark. The ark was the highest symbol of propitiatory prayer in the tabernacle. The death occurred when God had to keep His word about His holiness (Numbers 4:15). None but priests could carry the ark, and they had to carry it, not on wagons, but on their shoulders. They were carrying "the ark of God, which is called by the name of the LORD of hosts who sits enthroned on the cherubim" (6:2). God is specific about honoring His name in all we do for Him. As they brought the ark (after the striking of Uzzah), the Israelites broke into celebratory prayer:

"David and all the house of Israel were celebrating before the LORD, with songs and lyres and harps and tambourines and castanets and cymbals" (6:5).

After the Uzzah incident, God blessed the house of Obed-edom while the ark lodged there, and so David brought the ark to "the city of David" with rejoicing (6:12). In David's ecstasy, he was dancing and shouting (6:14,16). At Michal's remonstrance, David justified his actions:

> It was before the LORD, who chose me above your father and above all his house, to appoint me as prince over Israel, the people of the LORD — and I will celebrate before the LORD. I will make myself yet more contemptible than this, and I will be abased in your eyes. (6:21-22)

Apparently, it was not beneath royalty to celebrate before the Lord with demonstrative prayer. The "sons of Korah" wrote, "Clap your hands, all peoples! Shout to God with loud songs of joy!" (Psalm 47:1). Later the psalmist cried, "Lift up your hands to the holy place and bless the LORD!" (Psalm 134:2). The climactic praise psalm even called for jubilant dancing: "Praise him with tambourine and dance; praise Him with strings and pipe!" (Psalm 150:4). While most of the significant prayers of the Bible show more reverence than exuberance, we must not despise demonstrations of joy before the Lord, always keeping in mind two cautions: that corporate excitement does not become a means of calling attention to oneself and that our clapping praises the Lord rather than a worship leader.

David's next prayer showed just the opposite; it modeled reverence as David praised the self-sufficient greatness of God who can dispose as He pleases (7:18-29). David "sat before the LORD" (7:18). His is the only example in the Bible where a person sits to pray. Sometimes people bowed and knelt (Philippians 2:10) or, more rarely, prayed prostrate on the ground (Isaiah 29:4; more often they prostrated themselves before rulers). The bodily position of prayer does not occupy the biblical writers' minds except to show humility, which emerges in David's prayer here inherently.

This prayer shows the same humility and reversal of circumstances that Hannah's prayer does. David's acknowledgement of God as source appeared when he dedicated to the Lord all that Joram brought him (8:11). David's obedient spirit was contagious; even Joab, facing the Arameans and Ammonites, prayed "May the LORD do what seems good to him" (10:12).

David once more inquired of the Lord about the fate of Bathsheba's baby (12:16). His change of countenance when the child died showed his submission to God (12:20). The Bible tells us that David even worshipped on this occasion.

Vows appear again in this section. Absalom made a false vow to David when he was planning to usurp the throne (15:7-8). He paid severe consequences. Joab swore by the Lord that David's troops would desert him when David mourned for Absalom — a true oath (19:7). Another example of a true vow occurs when Ittai assured the king that he (Ittai) would not desert David, "as the LORD lives" (15:21). Since Ittai was a Philistine, this was a striking example of loyalty to the true God.

David once again inquired of the Lord about justice for Saul's treatment of the Gibeonites. Inquiring of the Lord is as characteristic of David in 2 Samuel as it is in 1 Samuel. David's nobility in prayer showed when he ordered a proper burial for Saul and Jonathan. "And after that God responded to the plea for the land" (21:14).

David showed his wisdom when the prophet Gad offered him one of three punishments for his self-important census. David told Gad he preferred the plague: "Let us fall into the hand of the LORD, for His mercy is great" (24:14). When the angel of the Lord was striking the people, David cried to the Lord, "Behold, I have sinned, and I have done wickedly. But these sheep, what have they done? Please let your hand be against me and against my father's house" (24:17).

David purchased property from Araunah (Ornan in 1 Chronicles). In reply to Araunah's offering of the land, David's perspicacious reply was, "I will not offer burnt offerings to the LORD my God that cost me nothing" (24:24). The book of 2 Samuel concludes with the announcement, "So the LORD responded to the plea for the land, and the plague was averted from Israel" (24:25). David prayed extensively throughout the whole process; the conclusion with an altar characterized his nobility.

David's qualities throughout the two books of Samuel foreshadow Christ's prayer life: David inquired of the Lord before moving, he was patient under the duress of Saul's and Absalom's persecutions, and he was honest and unselfish in deflecting God's punishment from the people to himself. It is small wonder that, with all his failures, David's character triumphed and God confirmed his prayers.

The outstanding celebration prayer in 2 Samuel is David's long paean to the Lord in 2 Samuel 22:1-51; he poured out a poem so worthy that it was repeated in Psalm 18. In this song of thanksgiving, David recounted how God answered when he called and he praised God for the blessings bestowed on the king.

The Books of the Kings

Both the Samuel and Kings books treat the northern and southern kingdoms, including all the wicked kings. The Chronicles deal only with the sacred history of the southern kingdom and do not deal with the northern kingdom. Bathsheba is not mentioned, although David's sinful census is (1 Chronicles 21:1-6).

Key Prayer Verses for 1 Kings

After Solomon's long prayer for the future of the nation, he appeals to God:

> Let these words of mine, with which I have pleaded before the LORD, be near to the LORD our God day and night, and may he maintain the cause of his servant and the cause of his people Israel, as each day requires, that all the peoples of the earth may know that the LORD is God; there is no other. (8:59-60)

Solomon's sincerity becomes obvious when he asks God to keep this prayer in mind day and night.

Side issues. Other issues surface in this book before the main prayer theme. We have seen false oaths and vows. First Kings opens with false worship. When Adonijah tried to seize the throne, he sacrificed sheep, oxen, and fattened cattle (1:9). Nathan thwarted Adonijah's plan. David's servants prayed for Solomon's reign (1:47), and David praised God for Solomon's coronation (1:48).

Two oaths occur in chapter 2, both by Solomon. He swore to eliminate Adonijah when Adonijah asked for Abishag (David's companion late in life to keep him warm). The second oath occurs when Shimei, who had cursed David, disobeyed his injunction not to leave Jerusalem and was executed.

One of the most famous prayers in this Bible book is Solomon's request for wisdom (3:9). Here he asked God to remember his prayer for the people, but later forgot his own prayer for wisdom. Solomon eventually multiplied horses and wives. It is sad to remember this poignant prayer (3:9) in the light of Solomon's last years.

Hiram of Tyre blessed the Lord when he heard of Solomon's plans to build the temple (5:7). The dedication of the temple was filled with blessing and prayer (8:22-53). This prayer of Solomon for the nation, the longest prayer in the Bible, is the prayer of a sovereign looking into all the possibilities of a distant future for

Israel as God's chosen people. In his prayer Solomon covered every conceivable contingency. He prayed against many possible natural disasters, on behalf of the people when they sinned and returned to God, for foreigners that they might know and fear the God of Israel, and for the people when they went into captivity because of sin. Solomon followed this judicious prayer by an elaborate ceremony of sacrifices. His far-reaching fame brought to Israel even the Queen of Sheba, who was also moved to praise the Lord for the Solomonic blessings (10:9).

KEY PRAYER THEME FOR 1 KINGS
The Prayers That Maintain Israel's Faithfulness to the Lord (17:1; 18:36-37)

The scene shifts in chapter 15 to the northern kingdom. The main prayer theme of this book does not appear until chapter 17. The northern kingdom does not have one righteous king, mainly because they shifted the center of worship away from Jerusalem and the temple, contrary to God's decrees.

Through the Lord, Elijah multiplied flour for the widow of Zarephath (a Gentile) and raised her son from the dead (17:9-24). God chose to use the Elijah-Elisha period to work a number of miracles, which no doubt involved prayer.

The central prayer in this latter part of 1 Kings converges on the difficult work of the prophets Elijah, Elisha, Micaiah, and other prophets (20:35-42) to maintain Israel's faithfulness to the Lord. First Kings 13:2 also marks the beginning of the "word of the Lord" coming to a prophet, which occurs repeatedly with the other prophets, who expressed, "Thus says the Lord." This obviously occurred in prayer.

Elijah's famous exploits on Carmel and Horeb and with Ahab and Jezebel are covered in all commentaries. Interestingly, when Elijah felt quite alone, the Lord informed him that He had left seven thousand in Israel—because the Lord had that number who had not "bowed to Baal, and every mouth that has not kissed him" (19:18). This will later be corroborated when the widow, a wife of a prophet, appealed to Elisha (2 Kings 4:1). We can understand Elijah's sense of isolation when none of the seven thousand came forward during his trials, but this assures us that regardless of appearances, the Lord has a remnant that is faithful to Him. The last prophetic announcement came when Micaiah countered the four hundred false prophets of Ahab. God realized His pronouncements against Ahab shortly in the next battle; Ahab tried to disguise himself, yet was killed.

KEY PRAYER VERSE FOR 2 KINGS

The author expressed the key prayer verse for this book when Sennacherib threatened Jerusalem. Hezekiah's powerful prayer ends,

> So now, O LORD our God, save us, please, from his hand, that all the kingdoms of the earth may know that you, O LORD, are God alone. (19:19)

All the great prayers and all the great pray-ers of the Bible were consistently more concerned with the honor and glory of God than they were with His gifts or His help.

KEY PRAYER THEME FOR 2 KINGS

Certainty of the Word of God According to His Prophets (1:10-12; 2:14-22; 3:17; 4:6,17,34; 5:14; 6:17-18)

God often speaks directly to His prophets. In the numerous miracles of Elijah and Elisha, we are not told whether the voice of God is in response to dialogue or to simple prayer by the prophets. What matters is that God allowed Elisha to see some of Elijah's miracles so that he would continue the work in faith.

Elijah challenged Ahaziah for consulting Baal-zebub (1:3). Twice Ahaziah sent a company of fifty men to capture Elijah, who called down fire from heaven on the men (1:9-12). After Elijah's ascent into heaven, Elisha was faithful to his training. In parting the waters of the Jordan, Elisha cried, "Where is the LORD, the God of Elijah?" (2:14).

The prophets in 2 Kings also began using prayer to call down miracles. Elijah's miracles are the best known. Elisha's first miracle was cleansing bad water with salt (2:20-22). The second was furnishing water overnight for Israel (3:14-20). Then he multiplied the oil for one of the wives of the prophets (4:6). Next he raised the Shunammite woman's son from the dead (4:35). To purify a contaminated stew, he threw some meal into it (4:41). He multiplied bread for the people (4:44), as Jesus later would do.

Elisha had Naaman wash in the Jordan seven times (5:14) to heal his leprosy. Elisha restored the floating ax head (6:6) to a man who had borrowed it. When the Aramean king was enraged at Elisha's supernatural knowledge of his activities, he sent an army to capture Elisha, who then blinded their eyes through prayer (6:18). The Aramean siege of Samaria caused a famine, which Elisha alleviated by having all the Aramean army flee. The Lord "showed" Elisha that Hazael would be the next king of Damascus (8:13); this indicates that much of Elisha's prayer must have been in dialogue.

The exceptional period of miracles during Elijah's and Elisha's ministry indicates they may have had a faith beyond that of most prophets, especially since they had to work against the unbelief of much of the northern kingdom. Later Paul said that "Abraham believed God, and it was counted to him as righteousness" (Romans 4:3). The great pray-ers we have encountered so far have been distinguished by such faith that they lived bringing God's will to earth (Joseph, Moses, Joshua, and others).

Jehoahaz, a northern kingdom ruler, began his reign wickedly, but under the punitive hand of the Lord he "sought the favor of the

LORD, and the LORD listened to him" (13:4). This is the only occasion that the Bible records a northern king praying.

On the other hand, prayer happened frequently in Judah. When Rabshakeh, a military officer in Sennacherib's army, threatened Jerusalem, Hezekiah went to the temple, spread the enemy's letter before the Lord, and prayed. Hezekiah began with praise and then pleaded with God to spare the city (19:14-20). The Lord answered by sending Isaiah with assurance that God would punish Sennacherib, king of Assyria.

Later, when Hezekiah was mortally ill, he prayed for the Lord to spare his life and referred God to his own record of service to Him. God answered, again through Isaiah, that he would add fifteen years to the king's life and that He would deliver the city from the king of Assyria. When Hezekiah asked for a sign, God made the shadow go back on the stairway. Evidently pleased with Hezekiah's faithfulness, God was generous when Hezekiah doubted.

Judah's downward plunge was momentarily halted by the devout King Josiah. When the Book of the Law was found in the temple, Josiah sent the priest Hilkiah to the prophetess Huldah to inquire of the Lord. Huldah assured Josiah that although the kingdom would come to an end, it would not happen in Josiah's time. After his repair of the temple, Josiah

> stood by the pillar and made a covenant before the LORD, to walk after the LORD and to keep his commandments and his testimonies and his statutes with all his heart and all his soul, to perform the words of this covenant that were written in this book. And all the people joined in the covenant. (23:3)

But it was too late. The many idolatrous kings had led Israel to an irreversible point. The kings following Josiah were equally idolatrous (with one brief period when Manasseh repented). First Israel (the northern kingdom) failed and now Judah had moved beyond hope.

KEY PRAYER VERSE FOR 1 CHRONICLES

The Chronicles are concerned only with the southern kingdom and mainly record its religious history. Bathsheba is not mentioned, although David's fateful census is; God had a lesson to teach through the latter. After David collected the contributions for building the temple, he prayed,

> But who am I, and what is my people, that we should be able thus to offer willingly? For all things come from you, and of your own have we given you. (29:14)

This key verse could well apply to all of David's reign.

Side issues. Jabez's famous prayer (4:10) for God's blessing has been echoed repeatedly by Christians in this day. In their war against four nations, Reuben, Gad, and the half-tribe of Manasseh cried out to the Lord and "he granted their urgent plea because they trusted in him" (5:20). The Levitical genealogies mention the priestly work of Aaron and his sons (6:49). David made a covenant with the nation "before the LORD" (11:3). Characteristically, when David's warriors brought him water from the well in Bethlehem he "poured it out to the LORD" (11:18). First Chronicles mentions his celebration when the ark was taken from the Philistines (13:8) and also his frequent inquiring of the Lord (14:10,13-15).

KEY PRAYER THEME FOR 1 CHRONICLES
Celebrating the Greatness of God (15:16; 16:4-36,37-43; 23:5,13; 25:3,7; 29:10-22)

Much of the material in the Chronicles was recorded in the Kings and recurs here, with a stronger emphasis on the role of God and of the priests.

The major prayer theme of 1 Chronicles, celebrating God's greatness, fits well, considering that David was the king. In 1 Kings 8, the commemoration of bringing the ark into Jerusalem had set a memorable high point. In 1 Chronicles, on that occasion, David "appointed some of the Levites as ministers before the ark of the LORD, to invoke, to thank, and to praise the LORD, the God of Israel" (16:4).

David wrote a moving thanksgiving for Asaph and his relatives to use in exalting the Lord (16:4-36); thanksgiving is mentioned three times in this psalm, as well as the holiness and splendor of God.

> With them were Heman and Jeduthun and the rest of those chosen and expressly named to give thanks to the LORD, for his steadfast love endures forever. Heman and Jeduthun had trumpets and cymbals for the music and instruments for sacred song. (16:41-42)

Thanksgiving would become a major theme in David's psalms. He never forgot where he came from and God's many ways of exalting him. His humility shows in the next chapter's prayer, "Who am I, O LORD God, and what is my house, that you have brought me thus far?" (17:16). God honored him as an example of the importance of acknowledging God as source in a humble manner.

Although David was forbidden to build the temple, he dedicated much of his wealth, acquisitions, and gifts to the later work of building the temple. David's dedication to the Lord was contagious; when Joab faced the Ammonites and Arameans, he appealed to the Lord (19:13). The writer recorded David's wisdom after his foolish census (discussed above in 2 Samuel) once again (21:1–22:1). In commissioning his son Solomon, David prayed, "Now, my son, may the LORD be with you, and may you succeed in building the house of the LORD your God" (22:11, HCSB).

The celebration theme emerges again in the next chapter, when David appointed four thousand gatekeepers with the instruments he had made for worship. The chronicler recorded that the priests were to minister to the Lord and to pronounce blessings on His name forever (23:13). The musicians, were to "offer praises to the LORD with the instruments that I have made for praise" (23:5). The celebration continued after the peoples' contributions to the temple (29:9).

David concluded that celebration with a lengthy prayer (not a psalm) that asked God to "keep forever such purposes and thoughts in the hearts of your people, and direct their hearts toward you" (29:18). To conclude the celebrative nature of the festivity, "they ate and drank before the LORD on that day with great gladness" (29:22).

Thanksgiving characterizes many of the Psalms (for example, 92:1-2); the psalmists almost always connected thanksgiving with praise. (We shall encounter thanksgiving again in the healing of the ten lepers — Luke 17:17-18).

KEY PRAYER VERSE FOR 2 CHRONICLES

The key prayer verse is well-known:

> [When catastrophe comes] if my people who are called by my name humble themselves, and pray and seek my face and turn from their wicked ways, then I will hear from heaven and will forgive their sin and heal their land. (7:14)

This crucial word from God comes after Solomon's great prayer dedicating the temple.

KEY PRAYER THEME FOR 2 CHRONICLES

God Conditioning His Blessing on Humble Prayer (1:10; 2:6; 6:1-42; 7:14; 13:14-18; 14:11-12; 15:2; 20:1-22; 32:20-23)

The Samuel and Kings books record much of the material in the two Chronicles. The best known is Solomon's prayer for wisdom (1:10). Solomon acted with humility in his letter to Hiram requesting materials and craftsmen: "But who is able to build a temple for Him, since even heaven and the highest heaven cannot contain Him?" (2:6, HCSB).

In the process of dedicating the temple, Solomon assembled all the leaders. They began with a service of praise that caused the glory of the Lord to fill the temple (5:11-14). Following the service, Solomon voiced his long prayer and humbly concluded, "Now, my God, please let Your eyes be open and Your ears attentive to the prayer of this place" (6:40, HCSB). In the next chapter, the king and people offered enormous sacrifices to the Lord and dedicated the temple. God appeared in a dream to Solomon and assured him of the answer to his prayer. Our key verse (7:14) occurs in this context.

Rehoboam's abandoning the law of God brought swift retribution from God. God answered Solomon's prayer when the people humbled themselves. God granted them a "little deliverance" from the hand of Shishak (12:1-12). When Jeroboam of Israel surrounded Abijah, the army cried out to the Lord, who gave them not only victory but enabled them to capture some of Jeroboam's cities.

Later Asa (mostly a good king), cried to the Lord "O LORD, there is none like you to help, between the mighty and the weak. Help us, O LORD our God, for we rely on you" (14:11). The prophet Azariah called on Asa to remove the idols from Judah. After Asa obeyed, God sent a great revival (15:1-18). In Asa's next battle with Baasha the king of Israel, he was not so wise; he called on the king of Aram for help instead of God. Hanani the seer rebuked him:

> For the eyes of the LORD run to and fro throughout the whole earth, to give strong support to those whose heart is blameless toward him. You have done foolishly in this, for from now on you will have wars. (16:9)

God endorsed His prophet's word: Asa had war until his death.

When the Moabites, Ammonites, and Meunites came against Jehoshapat, he sought the Lord and proclaimed a fast (20:3). To give God a reason for protecting Judah, Jehoshaphat rehearsed God's previous kindnesses to the southern nation (20:6-9). He concluded his prayer with great wisdom: "We do not know what to do, but our eyes are on you" (20:12) — precisely the humility Solomon had mentioned in his dedication prayer. This should teach modern Christians that our present-day technology may be less a help than God. Jahaziel assured the nation that "the battle is not yours but God's" (20:15). God scattered the enemies in mutual conflict with one another. When they fled, Judah was three days gathering up the booty they left.

After Athaliah's death, the priest Jehoiada purified the temple and appointed priests to make the appropriate sacrifices, "with rejoicing and song ordained by David" (23:18, HCSB). Hezekiah also purified the temple and offered sacrifices. After the music they "bowed themselves and worshiped" (29:27-30). Following that, Hezekiah ordered the commemoration of the Passover. Couriers carrying the news of the celebration announced to the citizens (in line again with Solomon's prayer), He "will not turn away his face from you, if you return to him" (30:9). In the midst of the festivities, "the priests and Levites were ashamed, so that they consecrated themselves and brought burnt offerings into the house of the LORD" (30:15). Many "unclean" people also celebrated, but Hezekiah prayed for all of them and avoided a mere legalistic return to the Lord. Second Kings records Hezekiah's prayer when Assyria invaded, as well as his prayer to recover from the boils and seeming threat of death.

Josiah was the last good king. He too purified the temple and ordered a Passover. Second Kings also reports the answer to his inquiry of the Lord and the answer by Huldah. The kings after Josiah were idolatrous and led to the captivity in Babylon.

The additions of the Chronicles material to that of the Kings material shows more clearly God's special concern for Judah (with the Messianic line of David). Subsequent kings follow Rehoboam's repeated pattern of apostasy and subsequent humbling of himself. God's constancy proved that He had led Solomon aright in his long prayer, in spite of Solomon's later mistakes. God remembers our prayers and often overrides our mistakes. We can trust a God who keeps His word and does not depend on formal perfection, but on our heart—a heart like David's. David was not perfect in performance but he had a perfect heart.

Chapter Six

EZRA, NEHEMIAH, ESTHER, JOB

Key Prayer Verse for Ezra

Ezra and Nehemiah constitute one book in the Hebrew Bible, but are divided in English Bibles. They see the return of many of the Israelites to Jerusalem in fulfillment of God's prophetic word to Jeremiah in Jeremiah 25:11-12. Jeremiah reserved his discussion of the return after seventy years until the book by his name. Prayers of confession are important in both books but see their inception in Ezra, where Ezra the priest leads, on behalf of the nation, their confession:

> O my God, I am ashamed and blush to lift my face to you, my God, for our iniquities have risen higher than our heads, and our guilt has mounted up to the heavens. (9:6)

Confession, which involves repentance, maintains such importance that it will recur several times throughout the Bible, including Psalm 51 and 1 John 1:9.

KEY PRAYER THEME FOR EZRA
Confession and Repentance (9:3-15; 10:1-6)

The book begins with Cyrus's edict for the captives to return to Jerusalem (1:3). The returnees gave generously for the rebuilding of the temple (2:68-69). The rebuilding stopped when Rehum and Shemshai protested to Artaxerxes. Tattenai wrote King Darius who searched the archives and not only permitted a new start on the building, but ordered the builders to request needed materials, and asked the Israelites to "offer sacrifices of pleasing aroma to the God of heaven and pray for the life of the king and his sons" (6:10, HCSB).

The exiles celebrated the dedication of the house (6:16) and immediately celebrated the Passover. Artaxerxes sent Ezra to gather materials for the temple and to be a judge for the people (7:25). Ezra attributed all this movement to God, offered a sublime prayer of praise, and gathered Israelite leaders to return with him (7:27-28). He proclaimed a fast so "that we might humble ourselves before our God, to seek from him a safe journey for ourselves" (8:21).

On his arrival, Ezra discovered that all the peoples had intermarried with the pagans of the area, and sat "appalled until the evening sacrifice," after which he offered an awe-inspiring confession (9:4-15) on behalf of the nation. When Ezra fell facedown at the end of this corporate prayer, the people resolved to put away their foreign wives, which would also involve the rejection of their false gods. He assembled Israelites from all of Judah and Benjamin and commanded them to confess their sins and disown their foreign families. Ezra appointed family leaders to deal with those who disobeyed, and the majority obeyed. The nation was being prepared to be a holy nation worthy of a new temple.

KEY PRAYER VERSES FOR NEHEMIAH

When Nehemiah restored the Law and the Festival of Booths, the Levites sang a praise-song worthy of their new beginning. The key verses come from the first two verses of this poem:

Stand up and bless the LORD your God from everlasting to everlasting. Blessed be your glorious name, which is exalted above all blessing and praise.

You are the LORD, you alone. You have made heaven, the heaven of heavens, with all their host, the earth and all that is on it, the seas and all that is in them; and you preserve all of them; and the host of heaven worships you. (9:5-6)

Ezra and Nehemiah

Ezra was a priest who led the first foray back to Israel. Nehemiah was a cupbearer to the king and became the governor of Israel. Both men treat confession with great reverence.

KEY PRAYER THEME FOR NEHEMIAH
God Is Above All

The sequence of God's revelation here of various kinds of prayer begins appropriately with a prayer theme that enters into our own prayer life—including the very position of our bodies—as our growth becomes such that He is above all. Standing indicates a reverence for who He is totally. Ezra attributed all his movement to God. He offered a sublime prayer of praise and gathered the Israelite leaders to return to Him above all (Ezra 7:27-28).

Although Ezra and Nehemiah are twin books, Nehemiah contains considerably more prayer than Ezra. This is the biblical plan: Only after the people were somewhat resettled back in the land were the officials able to reinstitute the various priestly duties and festivals properly. Much of the prayer in Nehemiah is by Levites.

Jeremiah had predicted seventy years of captivity. Possibly these years date from the original deportation in 605 BC to Cyrus's first decree for their return. It seems more likely that they date from the destruction of the temple in 586 BC (eliminating all hope for a reinstitution of Yahweh-worship) to the dedication of the new temple in 516 BC. If the latter is true, the end of Jeremiah's seventy years occurred when Nehemiah prayed about the regathering of the captives to rebuild the wall and his appeal to the king to allow him to return to Jerusalem (1:5-11). Nehemiah was interceding for an event that God had prophesied would take place in that very year! He requested to go even though God had already said that the return would take place. Ezra and the earlier captives had not prayed such a prayer, and their condition, as described in Nehemiah's prayer, indicates that they hardly had a national consciousness.

Nehemiah's approach to Artaxerxes showed courage. He occupied the high position of cupbearer and he bravely approached the king with a sad face. The king granted his request and, once in Jerusalem, Nehemiah began the work of building the wall. The work was opposed by Sanballat, Tobiah, Arabs, Ammonites, and Ashdodites, so Nehemiah prayed (4:9), stationed a guard, and divided the men into two groups—a group of builders and a group of armed warriors. They worked with the reassurance that Jeremiah's prophecy was coming true—that God partnered with them in their prayer and work.

When some of the countrymen demanded usury from their fellows, Nehemiah elicited a promise that they would stop. He commissioned the priests to guard against breaking an oath that had been secured illicitly, then required an oath of loyalty from them and prayed, "May God shake out every man from his house and from his labor who does not keep this promise" (5:13). Nehemiah prayed, "Remember for my good, O my God, all that I have done for this people" (5:19). He responded bravely to their intimidation and prayed, "But now, O God, strengthen my hands" (6:9).

To restore national identity, Ezra read from the Book of the Law for an entire day. "Ezra blessed the LORD, the great God, and all the people answered, 'Amen, Amen,' lifting up their hands. And they bowed their heads and worshiped the LORD with their faces to the ground" (8:6).

As they grieved for their sins corporately, Ezra and Nehemiah told them, "And do not be grieved, for the joy of the LORD is your strength" (8:10).

The national confession of sin followed the Festival of Booths and contained what a confession should contain—a recitation of the specific sins that had brought about the captivity (9:16-31). The Levites began with the praise that is the key verse for this book (9:5-6). The leaders with their families made a detailed vow to keep the Law (10:30-39). In the enumeration of the Levites, Mattaniah began the thanksgiving in prayer (11:17) and Hashabiah, Sherebiah, and Jeshua with corresponding Levites opposite them, stood "to praise and to give thanks" (12:24).

At the dedication of the wall, one group of Levites proceeded to the left and one to the right, singing and playing instruments (12:27-43). The Levites celebrated "with gladness, with thanksgivings and with singing, with cymbals, harps, and lyres" (12:27). As the celebration ended, "they offered great sacrifices that day and rejoiced, for God had made them rejoice with great joy" (12:43). On this occasion "the women and children also rejoiced. And the joy of Jerusalem was heard far away" (12:43).

KEY PRAYER VERSE FOR ESTHER

This famous story has Esther bravely stating to Mordecai,

> Go and assemble all the Jews who can be found in Susa and fast for me. Don't eat or drink for three days, day or night. I and my female servants will also fast in the same way. (4:16, HCSB)

KEY PRAYER THEME FOR ESTHER

Fasting and Prayer

Fasting accompanies prayer throughout the Bible, as in Nehemiah's fasting in Nehemiah 1:4. Although the book of Esther does not mention prayer as such, the fasts almost certainly included prayer. After

Ahasuerus's decree to eliminate the Jews, they proceeded "with fasting and weeping and lamenting, and many of them lay in sackcloth and ashes" (4:3). This fasting was in connection with mourning.

Mordecai, Esther's cousin and guardian, advised her to go to the king. Her reply has echoed down through the centuries. It was against the law to approach the king without his summoning, but Esther agreed with the immortal words, "If I perish, I perish" (4:16). She and her maidens and all of Jewry fasted. They almost certainly prayed. It was then that her design exposed Haman's scheme, and the Jews were saved. This breathtaking story instituted the Feast of Purim. God used fasting and prayer to deliver a nation.

KEY PRAYER VERSE FOR JOB

In this story, as famous as that of Esther, a suffering innocent victim cried,

> Naked I came from my mother's womb, and naked shall I return. The LORD gave, and the LORD has taken away; blessed be the name of the LORD. (1:21)

Job intermingled his story with continuing "yets":

> Even after my skin has been destroyed, yet I will see God in my flesh. (19:26, HCSB)

> Though he slay me, I will hope in him;
>   yet I will argue my ways to his face. (13:15)

KEY PRAYER THEME FOR JOB
Pleading with God (6:8-10; 10:1-22; 13:3,20-28; 14:13-22)

Prior to his series of tragedies, "[Job] was a man . . . blameless and upright, one who feared God and turned away from evil" (1:1). The key verse above demonstrates Job's character after the first test. After the second test, his wife urged him to curse God and die. Job's answer, after the crushing attack on his health, was "Shall we receive good from God, and shall we not receive evil?" (2:10).

The platitudes of his friends throughout the book have remained meaningless truisms for many other "friends" down through the centuries. According to popular but unvoiced opinion, God did a "poor job in not first creating heaven" (with no proving ground for His own people). Job tried repeatedly to rebuff his friends' inane censure not with anger but with seemingly fruitless turning to God. Job did not pray with anger against God, but pleaded for God to hear him.

Inevitably, Job had complaints about his plight. He wished he had never been born (3:1-19). He wanted to die (6:8-10) and came close to blaming God in 10:1-22. He prayed that God would "let not dread of you terrify me" (13:21). He could not understand God's failure to answer him (30:20). In the strongest of his many laments, he cried in agony to God, "You have turned cruel to me; with the might of your hand you persecute me" (30:21). Yet in all his cries, the most constant complaint remained on God's failure to hear (31:35 and others). Job did not doubt God's integrity; he merely could not understand it.

On the other hand, in response to Bildad, Job praised God in His mighty creation (9:1-12). He did the same later in 26:7-14. In one of his responses to Zophar, he recognized platitudes for what they were: "Will you show partiality toward him? Will you plead the case for God?" (13:8). In another memorable response to Bildad, Job answered with a faith extraordinary in his circumstances:

> For I know that my Redeemer lives,
>> and at the last he will stand upon the earth.
> And after my skin has been thus destroyed,
>> yet in my flesh I shall see God,

whom I shall see for myself,
>   and my eyes shall behold, and not another. (19:25-27)

His faith also echoed in a later answer to Eliphaz:

But he knows the way that I take;
>   when he has tried me, I shall come out as gold.
My foot has held fast to his steps;
>   I have kept his way and have not turned aside.
I have not departed from the commandment of his lips;
>   I have treasured the words of his mouth more than my portion
>   of food. (23:10-12)

These words, scattered through the book, demonstrate that Job never fully departed from the outlook in the key prayer verse above (1:21).

Job's prayers were a constant cry for God to heed him:

Oh that I might have my request,
>   and that God would fulfill my hope. (6:8)

He realized that no one can argue with God:

If one wished to contend with him,
>   one could not answer him once in a thousand times. (9:3)

After Eliphaz's tirade, Job cried,

Oh, that I knew where I might find him,
>   that I might come even to his seat!
I would lay my case before him
>   and fill my mouth with arguments. (23:3-4)

It took only one word from God (40:2) to silence Job's pleas. God did not answer Job's questions; *He reveals Himself*—the ultimate answer to all questions. Job immediately repented and set things straight (40:4-5). Then God silenced the "friends": "My anger burns against you and against your two friends, for you have not spoken of me what is right, as my servant Job has" (42:7).

Although it seemed to Job that God was not listening, God had heard every word. God credited Job with truthfulness, and his cry for God to hear him. God's silence may seem to have lasted a long time, but time means nothing to God, who proved Job through trial and silence.

God tested Abraham with the demand that He sacrifice Isaac. God tested Job. May the Lord grant that our tests *prove* God's integrity, rightness, and holiness.

Chapter Seven

PSALMS, PROVERBS, ECCLESIASTES, SONG OF SOLOMON

KEY PRAYER VERSE FOR PSALMS

The psalms have so many varied themes that no one verse can be "key" to the inclusive topics. Most of the psalms are prayers. In view of the preponderance of praise, we might consider a praise verse to be the key to the many subjects covered, especially in view of the many psalms that indicate trust in difficult circumstances. The "shortcut" key verse for the book is:

> Hallelujah!
> How good it is to sing to our God,
> for praise is pleasant and lovely. (147:1, HCSB)

To help the reader, I have divided some of the major topics into categories. For each section, I have suggested key verses.

KEY PRAYER THEMES FOR PSALMS
Turning to God in All Circumstances

The key prayer theme throughout the book is turning to God in all circumstances. Because those circumstances are so varied, it seems appropriate to list the majority with *illustrations* of each one. The meanings that I will give each one are so transparent that in most cases, commentary is superfluous.

I originally divided the various themes of the many psalms, but it seemed bulky. I ultimately arrived at seventeen overarching topics, and even then, some of the classifications remain somewhat conditional. Some of the psalms include several topics in a single poem. Several of the editors in various translations assigned two headings to some of them. In rare cases, one psalm is listed below under two headings.

Modern readers may have difficulty with many of these themes because we do not easily transport ourselves into the ancient Jewish mindset. However, like us, Job and some of the psalmists wanted explanations. Ancient Jews came to realize that God does not explain Himself; He reveals Himself. The psalmists often appealed to God to "hear." Repeatedly, God shows us and the ancients that His revelation satisfies all that we need to know.

The psalmists, with all their questioning, never lost sight of the fact that God remained in control. In all their begging for refuge and protection, the poets inevitably turned to God. We can learn that from the psalms.

The psalmists saw opposition to God as foolish and often cried out for mercy. They continually cried for the presence and action of God, regardless of circumstances. They prayed in the confidence that God alone could vindicate them in their various predicaments. They also saw opposition to God's people as opposition to God Himself.

In addition to such dependence, the psalmists longed for God above all else; the songs are marked by intense desire for God. The poets were so accustomed to the presence of the Lord that they missed Him when God seemed to turn away. Humility, care for the poor, jealousy for the name of God, and high praise characterize the psalms.

The Ways of God (68, 78, 92, 107, 112, 124, 125, 131)

> Yet he, being compassionate,
>> atoned for their iniquity
>> and did not destroy them;
> he restrained his anger often
>> and did not stir up all his wrath. (78:38)

Many of the psalms recounting history also indicate the ways of God as He dealt with Israel. These various viewpoints are subsumed also under other categories, but they illustrate the several means God used to deal with His people and His adversaries.

Facing Adversaries (3, 94)

In Psalm 3, David cried a profound complaint; the subtitle reads "A Psalm of David, when he fled from Absalom his son." Note David's confidence in God in dire straits.

> O Lord, how many are my foes!
>> Many are rising against me. (3:1)

> But you, O Lord, are a shield about me,
>> my glory, and the lifter of my head. (3:3)

> Salvation belongs to the Lord;
>> your blessing be on your people! (3:8)

Seeming Dominance of the Wicked (12, 58)

> Save, O LORD, for the godly one is gone;
>> for the faithful have vanished from among the children of
>> man. (12:1)

> You, O LORD, will keep them;
>> you will guard us from this generation forever. (12:7)

> On every side the wicked prowl,
>> as vileness is exalted among the children of man. (12:8)

Cry for Vengeance (34, 94)

> O LORD, God of vengeance,
>> O God of vengeance, shine forth!
> Rise up, O judge of the earth;
>> repay to the proud what they deserve! (94:1-2)

Seeking Refuge (7, 11, 16, 18, 31, 56, 57, 59, 90, 91)

> In you, O LORD, do I take refuge;
>> let me never be put to shame;
>> in your righteousness deliver me! (31:1)

The Lord as refuge is often called a "Rock" (18:2) or a "Fortress" (91:2) or some other figure of speech. Such trust will be seen in many of the passages below.

Seeking God in Himself (throughout most of the psalms)

> O God, you are my God; earnestly I seek you;
>> my soul thirsts for you;

my flesh faints for you,
> as in a dry and weary land where there is no water. (63:1)

Because your steadfast love is better than life,
> my lips will praise you. (63:3)

Hunger and Thirst for God (42, 63, 84)

As a deer pants for flowing streams,
> so pants my soul for you, O God.
My soul thirsts for God,
> for the living God..
When shall I come and appear before God? (42:1-2)

Absolute Trust (23, 62, 115, 120, 135)

Whatever the LORD pleases, he does,
> in heaven and on earth,
> in the seas and all deeps. (135:6)

The implication of the many times in which the psalmists indicated God's freedom of will is that whatever God does is always right and suitable for them.

Wisdom (1, 14, 15, 37, 39, 41, 49, 73, 127, 133, 139)

The psalmist, like the writer of Proverbs, sought wisdom:

Search me, O God, and know my heart!
> Try me and know my thoughts!
And see if there be any grievous way in me,
> and lead me in the way everlasting! (139:23-24)

Because the wisdom psalms were sung in the temple, they may be considered a kind of prayer, always conscious of God even though address to Him may seem secondary.

Thanksgiving (9, 21, 40, 75, 105, 116, 118, 126)

> I will give thanks to the LORD with my whole heart;
>> I will recount all of your wonderful deeds. (9:1)

Thanksgiving grows out of trust and in the psalms, thanksgiving and trust often are intertwined, as in Psalm 9. Thanksgiving is an important kind of prayer because it indicates our dependence on God. We are acknowledging our lowly need of Him, which is an important aspect of our relationship to Him. All prayer ultimately indicates a relationship with God, and thanksgiving especially draws us closer to Him. Thanksgiving permeates a majority of the New Testament letters.

In my prayers, I acknowledge that I can see only partially. I ask God to make my gratitude for the nameable and knowable a token of the vast unknown and unnameable blessings that I am unable to specify.

God's Revelation of Himself (19, 119)

The psalmist did not depend on himself to know God's ways; he depended on God.

> Teach me, O LORD, the way of your statutes;
>> and I will keep it to the end. (119:33)

Psalm 19 is a revelation of God in nature, as is much of Psalm 104 (and Romans 1). Psalm 119 dwells on God's revealing Himself through His word.

Plea for God to Heed (4, 5, 17, 20, 25, 27, 28, 35, 39, 55, 83, 86, 102, 109, 123, 143)

> Answer me when I call, O God of my righteousness!
>> You have given me relief when I was in distress.
>> Be gracious to me and hear my prayer! (4:1)

These prayers remind us of Job's repeated cries for God to listen. It is comforting to realize that many of the great saints of the Bible (people like us) cried for God to hear their prayer. When you are desperate, try one of these great poems as your prayer. God's seeming indifference to our prayer is one of His means of getting us to cry to Him. Even a cry to God is better than apathy. At least we are aware that all power comes from Him.

Plea for God to Help (10, 12, 13, 60, 70, 79, 80, 82, 104, 114, 117, 140, 142)

Notice that in this key verse, the psalmist asked God to "make haste," so it is legitimate at times to ask God to hurry!

> Make haste, O God, to deliver me!
>> O LORD, make haste to help me! (70:1)

These prayers emphasize the utter helplessness of the pray-er. He has no one or no other available help, except from God. We can be grateful that the Holy Spirit included these prayers for our use.

Penitential Psalms (6, 32, 38, 51, 102, 143; it is helpful also to include 106 and 137)

As their title suggests, these are psalms of repentance, and all except 137 include an assurance of forgiveness or an appeal with ensuing hope for God to spare the pray-er of the consequences of his or her own sin.

For centuries Christians have been dismayed at the occasional bitter spirit that creeps into the penitential psalms and even an occasional cry for vengeance. It must be remembered that not until Jesus was the law "fulfilled," and the higher noble spirit of the New Testament was not yet fully understood. These cries for retribution, even the most bitter of them, may indicate an identification with God's wrath on unholiness. In view of the teaching of Jesus, we may use these psalms for instruction or for insight into the Jewish mindset, sometimes closely identified with the divine mindset.

Nevertheless, it is dangerous business to think we can identify our finite comprehension with the infinite mind of immeasurable nobility. The one prayer available to us is a cry for justice, but not in anger or in a vengeful spirit. We are even to love our enemies, a high and difficult calling but one available even to Joseph with his brothers.

Psalm 51 is a plea for forgiveness. David's cry for mercy is on the basis of God's steadfast love. David based his prayer on the basis of an inner change:

> The sacrifices of God are a broken spirit;
>> a broken and contrite heart, O God, you will not despise. (51:17)

Psalm 38 instructs us further in confession and Psalm 32 deals with the joy that accompanies forgiveness.

Messianic **(2, 22, 72, 110, and occasional hints in many others)**
A number of the psalms indicate a clear foreview of the Messiah:

> I will tell of the decree:
> The LORD said to me, "You are my Son;
>> today I have begotten you.
> Ask of me, and I will make the nations your heritage,
>> and the ends of the earth your possession. (2:7-8)

The greatest scholars have pointed out Messianic indications in many of the psalms, but here it seems appropriate to list only those psalms most commonly called Messianic. Psalms 2 and 72 deal with Messiah's reign. Psalm 22 treats His suffering. Psalm 110 describes His power. These psalms are frequently quoted in the New Testament.

The Book of Praises

The Hebrew title of the Psalms literally means "praises," and the main content of the book is praise to God. The Songs of Ascents were praises. The psalm book was the hymnbook of the temple. The praises varied greatly in content and vocabulary. Many of our modern English words used in our hymns and songs derive directly from the psalms. Formerly, the psalm book was the main hymnal of the church.

Praising and Blessing the Lord (29, 33, 34, 45, 66, 67, 87, 89, 93, 95, 96, 97, 98, 99, 101, 103, 108, 111, 113, 121, 122, 129, 132, 134, 144, 145, 146, 147, 148, 149, 150)
Obviously, from the number in the list above, praise is the main theme of the psalms. This key verse is only representative.

Let everything that has breath praise the LORD! (150:6)

As to be expected in the hymnbook for the temple, the praise psalms dominate all categories. The term *Hallelujah* ("You praise the Lord") occurs twenty-four times in the Psalter. The term "the Great Hallel" is most often applied to Psalms 120–134, although some dictionaries include others in the group. Psalms 120–134 are also called "Songs of Ascents." Various scholars attribute that name to different sources. The most common explanation seems to be that as the pilgrims approached Jerusalem for one of the festivals, they sang them.

A few factors run through all the psalms, different as they are. One can discern trust in all of them in various degrees, even the penitential psalms. All the cries for help indicate a faith in the one trustworthy source, who is omnipotent as well as generous.

The psalms make it clear that God expects openness and honesty from us. None of the psalms exhibit false piety or even faith when all that makes for faith has been damaged. (It almost seems strange that some of the psalms could have been sung in the temple.) The psalmists make no disguise when they are embittered.

The psalms always demonstrate intensity. When they are full of complaint, one can feel the tears. When they are full of praise, we feel lifted up, regardless of our condition. When they are a cry for help, we identify so strongly that the cry becomes our own. In a day of much indifference to the human condition or to our own present condition, we turn to the psalms.

The psalms were sung. Frequently they designate a particular tune or an instrument to accompany them. The Hebrews were a musical people — David, Jeduthun, Heman, Asaph, the sons of Korah (probably), and many others are named as musicians.

The psalms are also poetry. The main poetic device used is parallelism. Discussions of the various kinds of parallelism can be found in almost any Bible dictionary. Briefly, some examples are:[1]

Synonymous

> The wicked will not stand in the judgment,
>> nor sinners in the congregation of the righteous. (1:5)

Synthetic

> God looks down from heaven
>> on the children of man
> to see if there are any who understand,
>> who seek after God. (53:2)

Antithetic

> The wicked plots against the righteous
>> and gnashes his teeth at him,
> but the Lord laughs at the wicked,
>> for he sees that his day is coming. (37:12-13)

Consequential

> The LORD is my shepherd; I shall not want. (23:1)

Climactic (or Stairlike)

> The LORD is my rock and my fortress and my deliverer,
>> my God, my rock, in whom I take refuge,
>> my shield, and the horn of my salvation, my stronghold. (18:2)

Chiastic (the parallel pattern is usually ABBA)

> If I forget you, O Jerusalem,
>> let my right hand forget its skill!
> Let my tongue stick to the roof of my mouth,
>> if I do not remember you,
> if I do not set Jerusalem
>> above my highest joy! (137:5-6)

Various dictionaries and books on Hebrew poetry add still other varieties and examples. The above six seem to be the most commonly named patterns.

Often the psalms were written in an acrostic form. Examples of acrostic psalms are 9, 10, 25, 34, 37, 111, 112, 119, 145, and, in the poetical books, Proverbs 31:10-31 and Lamentations 1–4. Both parallelism and acrostic form would make the poetry easy to memorize. Moreover, parallelism can be translated into any language without loss of meaning. Poetic form heightens the power of the biblical insights. This is why praise dominates the psalms.

Most important of all, the psalms reveal the nature of God. Almost every historical narration and praise song reveals new attributes of God. They often expound especially on His omniscience, omnipresence, greatness, and wisdom in many and various ways.

The enthusiasm of the psalmists reveals many names of God. The most common are simply "LORD" and "God." Even these are expanded: "the LORD, the Most High" (47:2), "God of my salvation" (88:1), "Yahweh" (143:11; usually translated "LORD") and "Adonai" (Lord) in various inflections, such as "LORD my God" (109:26). So many other names are frequently repeated that only one example of each of the following will be given: "Shield" (3:3), "Strength" (46:1), "Most High" (87:5), "Refuge" (90:1, HCSB), "Fortress" (91:2), "King" (95:3), "Maker of heaven and earth" (115:15, HCSB), "the One enthroned in heaven" (123:1, HCSB), and "Rock" (144:1).

The Bible is especially precious to followers of Christ, and the psalms are a peculiar treasure trove for Christians. Poetry is scattered all through the Bible, but here is a collection gathered together that seems inexhaustible in every kind of eminence available to human language.

KEY PRAYER VERSE FOR PROVERBS

Like the psalms, the proverbs have an enormous variety of meanings and insights. For the purpose of prayer, perhaps the middle of the book gives us the most evocative:

The LORD is far from the wicked,
> but he hears the prayer of the righteous. (15:29)

Note the antithetical form — very easy to grasp.

KEY PRAYER THEME FOR PROVERBS
The Lord Hears the Righteous (1:28-29; 15:8,29; 28:9,13)

This Wisdom book was not normally to be sung in the temple, and consequently, we find no overt prose prayer in it. Among so many aphorisms, inevitably we find several that subtly teach on prayer. Since the Wisdom books are concerned with various elements of righteousness, all the proverbs listed above inform us that God does not hear the prayer of the wicked, but of the righteous. That is the prayer theme for the proverbs. A typical example (other than the key verse above) is:

> If one turns away his ear from hearing the law,
> even his prayer is an abomination. (28:9)

The law, of course, defined what was "righteousness."

KEY PRAYER VERSE FOR ECCLESIASTES
The key verse for this book is:

> Be not rash with your mouth, nor let your heart be hasty to utter a word before God, for God is in heaven and you are on earth. Therefore let your words be few. (5:2)

As concise as this verse is, it has been one of the most helpful verses in the Bible for my own prayers. Prayer cannot be a performance or even the legal fulfillment of an obligation. We cannot address any higher nobility and majesty than God Himself. I begin my personal "quiet time" by praising God and meditating on His attributes. This helps orient me to God's greatness and His infinity.

KEY PRAYER THEME FOR ECCLESIASTES
Be Judicious in Prayer (5:2,4-5)
The intercession part of my prayer is perhaps the most awkward part of my day. I find myself cautious and I attempt to be judicious in the awareness that I am addressing the ultimate nobility of the universe. I never forget my limitations when I am asking God for anything.

The key prayer verse above orients us to the wisdom of the preacher. Later he warns us of another danger in prayer: "When you vow a vow to God, do not delay paying it, for he has no pleasure in fools. Pay what you vow. It is better that you should not vow than that you should vow and not pay" (5:4-5).

Since we live in a day of careless vows, we would be wise to heed this caution.

KEY PRAYER VERSE FOR SONG OF SOLOMON
This love song has had many interpretations. It is summarized in the key verse:

> I am my beloved's,
> and his desire is for me. (7:10)

KEY PRAYER THEME FOR SONG OF SOLOMON
Exceeding Love (1:4; 2:2; 5:10; 8:14; and others)
This sensual love song has been variously interpreted down through the centuries. Some commentators see in it a love-dialogue between Yahweh and Israel, others as a picture of the mutual love of Christ and His church. Whatever interpretation you choose, all see it (1) as

a perfect picture of mutual love and (2) as the speakers in that kind of dialogue. It is evident that God intended us to understand the two-sidedness of His love for us and our love for Him. The key "prayer" theme is that lovers want to dialogue. We have seen several instances of prayer-dialogue between God and humans (Moses and God, Gideon and God). God wants us to know that prayer (our relationship with Him) is not one-sided.

> Draw me after you; let us run.
>> The king has brought me into his chambers. (1:4)

> As a lily among brambles,
>> so is my love among the young women. (2:2)

> My beloved is radiant and ruddy,
>> distinguished among ten thousand. (5:10)

The sensuality in this poem is at places shocking. Once again, the writer used seemingly extreme language to picture the love that God wants us to experience. God *is* love (1 John 4:8,16) and if we grow in Christlikeness, we ourselves may *become* love as the basic nature of our being.

Chapter Eight

ISAIAH, JEREMIAH, LAMENTATIONS

KEY PRAYER VERSE FOR ISAIAH

God, being omniscient, knows what we are going to pray before we voice our words to Him. Because He knows all our prayers, past and future, we can pray retrospectively, presently, and prospectively. Sometimes during the day I will remember an important item I forgot to pray about in my early morning quiet time, and I will pray that, retrospectively, God helped John on his test that morning. Prospectively, I may pray about something in the immediate or distant future. Or, quite often, I pray that God will make His will clear enough to me that I can provide Him with the tool, the aroma of my prayer, in time for me to work under His direction about something far into the future. We exist in time; God is in eternity, and wants us to pray in our present tense as He leads us. Isaiah voices God's willingness to answer:

> Before they call I will answer;
> while they are yet speaking I will hear (65:24).

With this promise, Isaiah summed up much of what God said to him throughout this book.

KEY PRAYER THEME FOR ISAIAH[1]

Isaiah begins with a strong rebuke for the insincere, sinful offerings in the festivals of Israel (1:11-15). Amos 5:21-23 bears a strong resemblance to this passage. Amos and Isaiah were near contemporaries; both served under Uzziah. In Isaiah, God warned,

> When you spread out your hands,
>> I will hide my eyes from you;
> even though you make many prayers,
>> I will not listen;
>> your hands are full of blood. (1:15)

However, in Isaiah, God immediately invited Israel to return to Him. He did not do that in Amos.

Responsiveness of God to His People (30:19; 37:4; 58:9; 63:9; 65:24)

Isaiah's key prayer theme revolves around God's responsiveness to His people. In the famous theophany of 6:1-13, God invited Isaiah, "Whom shall I send, and who will go for us?" (6:8). Even though God's message becomes one of doom, He included His prophet in His plan to speak to Israel.

When Judah was threatened by Aram and Israel, God kindly invited King Ahaz to ask for a sign, which Ahaz refused (7:1-13). Isaiah told Ahaz that God would give the following sign: a virgin would conceive and bear a son called "Immanuel" (7:14). Centuries later God would apply this prophecy to the young virgin Mary, and at that time God Himself would walk among men (Matthew 1:18-23). God hinted at this future meaning in addressing the prophecy to the "house of David" (7:13).

After another promise of deliverance (11:11) Isaiah produced a psalm of thanksgiving that also indicated God's care for Israel in spite of her sins:

> I will give thanks to you, O LORD,
>> for though you were angry with me,
> your anger turned away,
>> that you might comfort me. (12:1)

After recounting God's blessings, Isaiah has three consecutive chapters of praise: 25, 26, and 27. In Isaiah 25, Israel staked her claim on God (verses 1-5, and then in verses 6-10, a series of promises for His people). In chapter 26, God was a rock who humbled the proud (verses 1-6) and then, in magnificent poetry, He assured Israel of His various means of protection (verses 7-21). Echoing David, the poet claimed, "You have . . . done for us all our works" (verse 12). Chapter 27 offers praise for God's protection, and then affirms that those lost in Assyria and dispersed in Egypt "will come and worship the LORD on the holy mountain at Jerusalem" (verse 13).

Chapters 28–30 are mostly a prolonged rebuke. God briefly interrupted His reprimand with a stirring promise:

> Behold, I am the one who has laid as a foundation in Zion,
>> a stone, a tested stone,
> a precious cornerstone, of a sure foundation:
>> "Whoever believes will not be in haste." (28:16)

He concluded with another example of His responsiveness to their condition:

> The LORD waits to be gracious to you,
>> and therefore he exalts himself to show mercy to you.

> For the LORD is a God of justice;
>> blessed are all those who wait for him. . . .

> And though the Lord give you the bread of adversity and the water
> of affliction, yet your Teacher will not hide himself anymore, but
> your eyes shall see your Teacher. And your ears shall hear a word
> behind you, saying, "This is the way, walk in it," when you turn to
> the right or when you turn to the left. (30:18,20-21)

When Sennacherib threatened Hezekiah, the king sent a plea to
Isaiah asking him to offer a prayer for the remnant in Jerusalem
(37:5). Rabshakeh's letter, Hezekiah's prayer, and God's answer were
discussed earlier in connection with 2 Kings 19 (see page 59). Isaiah
also records Hezekiah's illness and recovery (chapter 38), but not
the remarkable sign that the author described in 2 Kings 20.

The latter part of Isaiah (42–53) contains four "servant songs."
In the remarkably prescient fourth servant song (52:13–53:12),
Isaiah ended the description of the suffering Messiah with the
words, "Yet He bore the sin of many and *interceded* for the rebels"
(53:12, HCSB, emphasis added). The Messiah's intercession is one
of the most reassuring prayers in the Bible. The New Testament
picks up on this in Hebrews 7:25; in 1 John 2:1, Jesus prayed for us
in our sin.

In Isaiah 55, Isaiah recorded a heartwarming invitation for the
thirsty to partake of God's wine and milk without cost. In the
middle of it, Isaiah advised, "Seek the LORD while He may be
found; call to Him while He is near" (55:6, HCSB). In the following
chapter, foreigners were invited to join the covenant, and God
promised,

> These I will bring to my holy mountain,
>> and make them joyful in my house of prayer;
> their burnt offerings and their sacrifices

will be accepted on my altar;
for my house shall be called a house of prayer
    for all peoples. (56:7)

Jesus Himself used these very words to drive out the money changers from the temple (Matthew 21:13; Mark 11:17; Luke 19:46). Isaiah 58 devotes an entire chapter on right fasting (with appropriate character and behavior) and wrong fasting (in insincerity, sin, and pride). In the latter case, the person fasting is trying to manipulate God; his prayer is superstition, rather than relationship. So fasting can be a help or a hindrance to our prayer.

Isaiah 59 reveals the cause of unanswered prayer: our iniquities (59:2). After enumerating some of Israel's sins, God "wondered that there was no one to intercede" (59:16). Isaiah added that God had to bring His own salvation and righteousness without the help that human prayer would have brought.

The Lord calls His own pray-ers:

On your walls, O Jerusalem,
    I have set watchmen;
all the day and all the night
    they shall never be silent.
You who put the LORD in remembrance,
    take no rest,
and give him no rest
    until he establishes Jerusalem
    and makes it a praise in the earth. (62:6-7)

Isaiah declared that God clearly reveals His own responsiveness to His people in one of the most poignant passages in Isaiah:

In all their affliction he was afflicted,
    and the angel of his presence saved them;

in his love and in his pity he redeemed them;
>he lifted them up and carried them all the days of old. (63:9)

After remembering some of God's feats from the past, Isaiah cried to the Lord, "Look down from heaven and see, from your holy and beautiful habitation" (63:15) and later he entreated, "Oh that you would rend the heavens and come down" (64:1). Isaiah began to sound almost like Job! But shortly he confessed,

But now, O Lord, you are our Father;
>we are the clay, and you are our potter;
>we are all the work of your hand. (64:8)

The prophet begged God not to be angry or remember their iniquity (64:9). And chapter 65 introduces that faithful promise that before they call, God will answer — our key verse for this book.

To keep Isaiah humble, God told him that heaven is His throne and earth is His footstool (66:1). To conclude Isaiah's revelation, God promised peace and wealth to the nations and an enduring new heavens and new earth (65:17; 66:22).

Isaiah and Jeremiah

In earlier days, I dreaded leaving the Alpine heights of Isaiah to enter the plaints of the weeping prophet. But if we are to be partakers of the divine nature (2 Peter 1:4), we may legitimately share the wrath of God against a rebellious people. We may even participate in that in judgment.

KEY PRAYER VERSE FOR JEREMIAH

Jeremiah was imprisoned when the Lord told him,

> Call to me and I will answer you, and will tell you great and hidden
> things that you have not known. (33:3)

God gave this as one of many assurances to a prophet lamenting
a fallen nation.

KEY PRAYER THEME FOR JEREMIAH

*The Pray-er's Helplessness in the Face of Human Will, Opposed to
Confident Faith in God's Will* (10:6-10; 11:18-23; 12:1-4; 17:14;
32:25-27)

All through the Old Testament, God tied the prayer of an individual
to the fate of the nation. Jeremiah made this more evident than any
other prophet. Early in Jeremiah, the prophet received a strange command from God:

> As for you, do not pray for this people, or lift up a cry or prayer
> for them, and do not intercede with me, for I will not hear you.
> (7:16)

This directive could have come only if Israel had so sinned that
they passed a point of no return. The heart-burning plaints of the
first nine chapters indicate the tears of the broken prophet.

The Lord boosted Jeremiah's spirits after such sorrow by reassuring Jeremiah of His own power and ultimacy (10:6-20). In his grief,
Jeremiah spoke of humanity's dependence on God:

> I know, O LORD, that the way of man is not in himself,
>   that it is not in man who walks to direct his steps. (10:23)

This is an echo of Psalm 37:23 and Proverbs 20:24. After reminding Jeremiah of his broken covenant, God again warned Jeremiah not to pray for Judah (11:14). When Jeremiah learned that the people of Anathoth were plotting against him, he appealed to the all-knowing Lord for vengeance on them (11:20). Jeremiah questioned God about why the wicked prosper (12:1), but appropriately appealed to God's knowledge of himself and his heart (12:3).

Following a burdensome drought, Jeremiah could not resist an appeal to the Lord:

> Though our iniquities testify against us,
>> act, O Lord, for your name's sake. . . .
> Yet you, O Lord, are in the midst of us,
>> and we are called by your name;
>> do not leave us. (14:7,9)

God once again warned Jeremiah, "Do not pray for the welfare of this people. Though they fast, I will not hear their cry" (14:11-12). Like Job, Jeremiah wished he had never been born (15:10). The prophet told God about his delight in God's word and that he was called by God's name (15:16). His calling may have been the most difficult calling in the Old Testament. God told the wailing prophet, "They shall turn to you, but you shall not turn to them" (15:19).

Jeremiah laid his woeful plight out before the Lord by reminding God of his faithfulness and again asked that his persecutors be put to shame (17:18). God and Jeremiah both reached the legitimate end of their patience when Jeremiah called down the wrath of God in 18:21-23. Jeremiah confessed that he could not help proclaiming God's word:

> If I say, "I will not mention him,
>> or speak any more in his name,"
> there is in my heart as it were a burning fire

> shut up in my bones,
> and I am weary with holding it in,
>   and I cannot. (20:9)

After the exile in Babylon, God told the exiles to settle there and "seek the welfare of the city where I have sent you into exile" (29:7). God, through the prophet, promised the deportees that after their return to Jerusalem in seventy years, "Then you will call upon me and come and pray to me, and I will hear you. You will seek me and find me, when you seek me with all your heart. I will be found by you, declares the LORD" (29:12-14). Joy and praise would accompany the restoration; God told them to sing, shout, proclaim, praise, and say, "O LORD, save your people" (31:7).

In a flashback to the time before the captivity, the Lord, knowing that Jeremiah was well aware of the coming captivity, told Jeremiah to buy a field in Anathoth. With such a preposterous command, Jeremiah confessed his faith: "Ah, Lord GOD! It is you who have made the heavens and the earth by your great power and by your outstretched arm! Nothing is too hard for you" (32:17).

Jeremiah affirmed his faith in 32:24. In Psalm 50:15 God had pledged to answer a call to Him and He repeated this affirmation in Jeremiah 32:27. In the next chapter, the Lord again asserted that His praise and worship would return to Jerusalem (33:10-11). He announced that the city would be filled with a sound of joy and gladness and the voices of bride and bridegroom:

> There shall be heard again the voice of mirth and the voice of gladness,
> the voice of the bridegroom and the voice of the bride, the voices of
> those who sing, as they bring thank offerings to the house of the LORD:
>
> "Give thanks to the LORD of hosts,
>   for the LORD is good,
>   for his steadfast love endures forever!" (33:10-11)

In chapter 36, Baruch transcribed all Jeremiah's words on a scroll, which he read in the temple. Jeremiah had hoped the people would repent and petition the Lord for help (36:7). However, the king, Jehoiakim, burned the scroll, so the prophet had to dictate it once again to Baruch. Zedekiah, Josiah's son and the last king, refused to obey Jeremiah's warning to obey the words of the Lord, but, nevertheless, the king sent the priests to ask Jeremiah to pray for them (37:3). God sent word back that the Israelites' helpers, the Egyptians, would return to Egypt and that the Chaldeans (Babylonians) would indeed take the city (37:7-10).

A series of intrigues followed in which the Babylonian appointee to the governorship was murdered. Johanan, a general, stepped in and asked Jeremiah to pray to the Lord for their work (42:2-3) and once again, God told Jeremiah to advise the people to stay in the land and not go to their Egyptian friends. They refused and took Jeremiah to Egypt with them, where they offended God by worshipping Egyptian gods. God therefore handed over Pharoah Hophra to his enemies. If the Judeans had remained in Israel, they would have had God's protection, but they fled to Egypt for their protection. What may seem to be right or judicious is wrong when it is a contradiction of the word of the Lord.

Of all the prophets, Jeremiah seems the bravest. He even dared, on rare occasions, to pray for Judah after God had forbidden such prayer. This lonely prophet stood against the people and all recognized authorities.

Jeremiah was the most steadfast of all the prophets. In spite of threats, imprisonments, being thrown into a cistern, and being an outcast, his first loyalty remained to God. His message never changed; he unswervingly stuck to the unpopular message that Judah should go with their captors to Babylon.

The remainder of Jeremiah is taken up with prophecies against Egypt, Philistia, Moab, Ammon, Edom, Kedar, Hazor, and Babylon. Jeremiah sent word to the Babylonians by Seraiah that Seraiah was to say, "LORD, You have threatened to cut off this place so that no one will live in it" (51:62, HCSB). He announced that a great cry (like the Exodus prayers) would go up from Babylon (51:54). The desolation of Babylon came some time after its defeat by the Persians.

KEY PRAYER VERSE FOR LAMENTATIONS

In spite of the gloominess of this book, cheeriness pervades the key verse:

> You came near when I called on you;
>> you said, "Do not fear!" (3:57)

Jeremiah's preceding prophetic book bears out the genuineness of his confidence. God stayed close to His prophet through tribulation and trial.

KEY PRAYER THEME FOR LAMENTATIONS
The Nearness of God in the Midst of Deep Trouble
(1:22; 3:37-39,55-56)

Poetry pervades the entire book, with two acrostics and a final poem. A prolonged lament occupies the verses on the fate of Jerusalem, with occasional inserts that demonstrate Jeremiah's unwavering faith in God. Probably Jeremiah intended most of the mourning for the ears of God. He prayed,

> Let all their evildoing come before you,
>> and deal with them
> as you have dealt with me
>> because of all my transgressions;
> for my groans are many,
>> and my heart is faint. (1:22)

His emotions show when he lamented,

My eyes are spent with weeping;
    my stomach churns;
my bile is poured out to the ground
    because of the destruction of the daughter of my people,
because infants and babies faint
    in the streets of the city. (2:11)

Yet he confidently sat astride his sorrow and proclaimed,

It is good that one should wait quietly
    for the salvation of the LORD. (3:26)

His confidence in the Lord never varied:

You have taken up my cause, O Lord;
    you have redeemed my life. (3:58)

Then he confidently poured out his assurance that God would repay his enemies (3:64). The entire last chapter is a long grief over the fate of the city; the poem appeals to the Lord to look upon the tragic situation:

Remember, O LORD, what has befallen us;
    look, and see our disgrace! (5:1)

Even in the middle of his dark pain, Jeremiah chose to identify both with God and His holiness and also with the people in their mourning.

Chapter Nine

EZEKIEL, DANIEL

KEY PRAYER VERSE FOR EZEKIEL

The key prayer verse for a book often comes only after God has established a basis for it. In Ezekiel, the key verse comes after the Lord has clearly stated the sins of Israel:

> Son of man, these men have taken their idols into their hearts, and
> set the stumbling block of their iniquity before their faces. Should
> I indeed let myself be consulted by them? (14:3)

KEY PRAYER THEME FOR EZEKIEL
God's Warning That Sin Hinders Prayer (14:3,7-8,12-13,19-20; 20:1-4)

Jeremiah seems complex because of the strange chronology and the various intrigues against him throughout his prophesying. He suffered greatly in his attempt to facilitate Israel's return to the Lord. Ezekiel also is complex, not because of intrigues, but because of his confusing and seemingly obscure visions and parables. His suffering was not from without (like Jeremiah's), but because of his jealousy for the holiness of the Lord. God had told Jeremiah not to pray for the people. Now in Ezekiel, God flatly stated that He will not hear their prayer: "My eye will not spare, nor will I have pity.

And though they cry in my ears with a loud voice, I will not hear them" (8:18).

As God's executioners carried out their grim task of killing the idolaters in the temple, Ezekiel cried to the Lord, "Ah, Lord GOD! Will you destroy all the remnant of Israel in the outpouring of your wrath on Jerusalem?" (9:8). Then Ezekiel witnessed the departing of God's glory from the temple and from Jerusalem (10:18-19). His suffering derived from heartbreak over Israel's rejection of Yahweh and Yahweh's various condemnations of their rebellion.

The Lord validated the strange visions Ezekiel has seen and later also the parables He gave Ezekiel. He condemned both the exiles and those in Jerusalem (chapters 11–12). After describing the anxiety of those in Israel and declaring their destruction because of their sin, He announced, "And you shall know that I am the LORD" (12:20), a knowledge not only from revelation but also from the extent of the Israelites' deserved suffering. The Lord decried the false prophecies as deceptive: "Thus says the Lord GOD, Woe to the foolish prophets who follow their own spirit, and have seen nothing!" (13:3). Ezekiel did not record the Israelites' praying during this period. He carried out the word of God in Isaiah on good and evil:

> Woe to those who call evil good
>   and good evil,
> who put darkness for light
>   and light for darkness,
> who put bitter for sweet
>   and sweet for bitter! (Isaiah 5:20)

In his anger, God informed Ezekiel, "Even if these three men, Noah, Daniel, and Job, were in it, they would deliver but their own lives by their righteousness" (14:14). Representative righteousness in the godly does not cover the sins of others. Elijah and Elisha did not deliver the northern kingdom. Jeremiah did not take away the sins of

Judah. And evidently even Ezekiel could not rescue the people from their own sins. Only Calvary can obliterate sin.

Even the prayer of inquiring of the Lord, so important in David's ministry, was forbidden. When the Israelite elders came to Ezekiel to inquire of the Lord, he declared the word of God:

> And the word of the LORD came to me: "Son of man, speak to the elders of Israel, and say to them, Thus says the Lord GOD, Is it to inquire of me that you come? As I live, declares the Lord GOD, I will not be inquired of by you." (20:2-3)

The end of the road had been reached after Josiah's death. Sin had so blinded the people of Judah that they did not realize it when they poured over the cliff of monstrous sin. Up to 36:1, through chapter after chapter, Ezekiel heard God's judgment, except for the brief passage on restoration in 20:33-44.

In the midst of all this condemnation, God told Ezekiel, "And I sought for a man among them who should build up the wall and stand in the breach before me for the land, that I should not destroy it, but I found none" (22:30).

God has a high view of intercession, because He "sought" for an intercessor. God had told Jeremiah not to pray for the people, and now even Ezekiel's intercession did not reach what God required, in view of the brazenness of Israel's sin. God's call to intercession required lofty and difficult effort, but God wanted it.

After condemning a series of nations (chapters 25–32), God appointed Ezekiel as a watchman over Israel (33:7) to call the people to repentance:

> "As I live," declares the Lord GOD, "I have no pleasure in the death of the wicked, but that the wicked turn from his way and live; turn back, turn back from your evil ways, for why will you die, O house of Israel?" (33:11; see 2 Peter 3:9)

The extraordinary patience of the Lord here indicates that God will catch us midway in our own fall. The return from exile indicates that with God, a final cutoff may be imminent, even if not foreseeable.

Chapter 36 begins a series of indications that God will indeed bring Israel back, including the description of the amazing valley of dry bones (chapter 37). God accurately described bringing back Israel to her own land; He would demonstrate His holiness through the returned peoples: "I will pour out My Spirit on the house of Israel" (39:25-29, especially 29, HCSB).

Ezekiel did not suffer the enormous persecution of Jeremiah but at times sounds like the priest that he was, offering hope to exiles. At the end of his glorious apocalypse, he magnificently told us that the name of that ultimate city will be "The LORD Is There" (48:35).

Twenty-first-century Christians need to take seriously the stern warnings of an offended God. Slowly the United States, Canada, and Europe are edging more and more into the sin of idolatry (1 Samuel 15:23). We need an Ezekiel today.

KEY PRAYER VERSE FOR DANIEL

When none of Nebuchadnezzar's wise men could interpret his frightening dream, Daniel urged his three friends, Hananiah, Mishael, and Azariah, to ask the God of heaven for mercy concerning the dream (2:18), since they, along with all the king's wise men, would be executed if they failed to accurately interpret the king's dream. When God revealed the mystery to Daniel, he praised the God of heaven and declared (our key verse),

> He reveals deep and hidden things;
>> he knows what is in the darkness,
>> and the light dwells with him. (2:22)

Nebuchadnezzar questioned Daniel, who told him that no human, medium, diviner-priest, or astrologer could fathom the dream or its meaning, "but there is a God in heaven who reveals mysteries, and he has made known to King Nebuchadnezzar what will be in the latter days" (2:28).

Daniel's Apocalypse

The New Testament writers and later interpreters have written much on Daniel 7 (see almost any commentary). Its concept of the Son of Man became Jesus' favorite designation for Himself. This vision is as challenging as the apocalypses in Ezekiel and Revelation.

KEY PRAYER THEME FOR DANIEL
Revelation of Hidden Things Through Prayer (2:17-19; 9:20-22; 10:12)

Daniel was careful to credit God with the revelation of the king's dream. Note that this revelation came through corporate prayer (Daniel and his three friends). (God also reveals apocalyptic visions in prayer in chapters 7–12.)

The oft-repeated tale of Shadrach, Meshach, and Abednego (Hananiah, Mishael, and Azariah) folds out the astounding story of incredible bravery as the three men refused to engage in false worship (false prayer). The story of their response to the king has echoed throughout history: "But if not, be it known to you, O king, that we will not serve your gods or worship the golden image that you have set up" (3:18). As they walked among the blazes, a fourth man who looked like "a son of the gods" (3:25) became visible. The men's deliverance from the fiery furnace even caused the king to praise their God and issue a command that no one should speak offensively against Him (3:29).

After Nebuchadnezzar's period of insanity, when his mind returned to normal, he once again praised the true God, even understanding the humility God was teaching him: "Now I, Nebuchadnezzar, praise and extol and honor the King of heaven, for all his works are right and his ways are just; and those who walk in pride he is able to humble" (4:37).

The incident of the lion's den under Darius the Mede shows Daniel once again crediting God with his deliverance (6:22). Daniel was praying to Yahweh when Darius's enemies tricked Darius into forbidding all prayer except to himself (6:1-28). Shadrach, Meshach, Abednego, and Daniel demonstrated more missionary spirit than their predecessors back in Israel had shown when Israel was free.

In the first year of Darius, Daniel, realizing that Jeremiah's seventy-year prophecy had been completed, spoke to the Lord, "Then I turned my face to the Lord God, seeking him by prayer and pleas for mercy with fasting and sackcloth and ashes" (9:3). In spite of knowing that God would carry out Jeremiah's prophecy, Daniel still prayed for the restoration of Jerusalem; he prayed for what he knew was going to happen! Daniel poured out an impassioned confession of the sins of Israel, with a plea that God forgive and have mercy on His destroyed sanctuary and His city (9:1-19).

God sent Gabriel with an answer to Daniel's prayer about the "seventy weeks" and the prophecy of a coming Messiah. In that, and in the apocalyptic visions that followed, an angel three times told Daniel he was "greatly loved" (9:23; 10:11,19).

After all the visions, the angel assured Daniel, "But go your way till the end. And you shall rest and shall stand in your allotted place at the end of the days" (12:13).

Some of the visions were terrifying, but Daniel could rest. The Bible records no sins of Daniel.

Chapter Ten

HOSEA THROUGH MALACHI

The Term *Minor*

These books are typically called "the minor prophets." The expression *minor prophets* does not mean "of lesser importance." It refers to the brevity of these important books. Some of the loftiest ideas in the Old Testament are found, for example, in Hosea and Habakkuk. We must take them as seriously as we take the longer books. They are still the word of God.

KEY PRAYER VERSE FOR HOSEA

This key verse comes toward the end of Hosea's long prophecy, which was largely a condemnation of Israel's infidelity. Through Hosea, God commanded,

> Take with you words
>   and return to the LORD;
> say to him,

"Take away all iniquity;
accept what is good,
        and we will pay with bulls
        the vows of our lips." (14:2)

Even after the dramatic picture in which God used the unfaithfulness of Gomer, Hosea's wife, to portray Israel's infidelity, God ended the book with an impressive invitation to return to Him.

KEY PRAYER THEME FOR HOSEA
Failure of the People to Pray (7:14; 11:7; 14:1-3)

God commanded Hosea to marry a promiscuous wife, Gomer.

Gomer was to Hosea what Israel was to God. This is the only prophetic book written by a northern prophet and for the northern kingdom, where spiritual prostitution was so rampant. The Lord described Israel's lack of true prayer vividly:

They do not cry to me from the heart,
        but they wail upon their beds;
for grain and wine they gash themselves;[1]
        they rebel against me. (7:14)

God also pointed out their hypocrisy in prayer:

To me they cry,
        "My God, we—Israel—know you."
Israel has spurned the good;
        the enemy shall pursue him. (8:2-3)

This theme of hypocrisy continues:

My people are bent on turning away from me,
>   and though they call out to the Most High,
>   he shall not raise them up at all. (11:7)

The final chapter is God's heartbreaking appeal for Israel to return to the Lord they had forsaken. From the history of the northern kingdom, we may conclude that Hosea's plea fell largely on deaf ears.

Key Prayer Verses for Joel

Two key prayer verses capture the prophet's intention for this short book. After the devastating locust plague, the Lord warned,

>   Rend your hearts and not your garments.
> Return to the Lord your God. (2:13)

Then a bit later Joel called out on behalf of God:

> Between the vestibule and the altar
>   let the priests, the ministers of the Lord, weep
> and say, "Spare your people, O Lord,
>   and make not your heritage a reproach,
>   a byword among the nations.
> Why should they say among the peoples,
>   'Where is their God?'" (2:17)

Key Prayer Theme for Joel
Our Desperate Need of Prayer (1:14,19-20; 2:13,17)

After describing the destruction caused by the locusts, Joel told the priests,

Consecrate a fast;
> call a solemn assembly.

Gather the elders
> and all the inhabitants of the land

to the house of the LORD your God,
> and cry out to the LORD. (1:14)

After a brief description of the terrifying Day of the Lord, Joel cried (again, note the many different kinds of cries in the prayers of the Bible),

To you, O LORD, I call.

For fire has devoured
> the pastures of the wilderness,

and flame has burned
> all the trees of the field. (1:19)

This frightening description is followed by the Lord's promise to restore Judah:

You shall eat in plenty and be satisfied,
> and praise the name of the LORD your God,
> who has dealt wondrously with you.

And my people shall never again be put to shame. (2:26)

After this promise, God added the promise of the Spirit and declared that everyone who calls on the name of Yahweh will be saved. He assured that security will be the heritage of those on Mount Zion and in Jerusalem: "Among the survivors shall be those whom the LORD calls" (2:32).

Joel ended his book with a judgment on the nations (3:1-16) and a promise of blessing on Israel, so typical of many of the prophetic books.

KEY PRAYER VERSES FOR AMOS

Curiously, God used a shepherd to censure the insincere worship of Judah. Samuel had warned,

> Has the LORD as great delight in burnt offerings and sacrifices,
> as in obeying the voice of the LORD?
> Behold, to obey is better than sacrifice,
> and to listen than the fat of rams. (1 Samuel 15:22)

Hosea also emphasized the spiritual nature of sincere worship. "For I desire steadfast love and not sacrifice, the knowledge of God rather than burnt offerings" (Hosea 6:6).

In spite of the prophets' directing the law toward spiritual purposes, now Amos has to quote the Lord (cited earlier in the commentary on Isaiah—see page 94):

> I hate, I despise your feasts,
> and I take no delight in your solemn assemblies.
> Even though you offer me your burnt offerings and grain offerings,
> I will not accept them;
> and the peace offerings of your fattened animals,
> I will not look upon them.
> Take away from me the noise of your songs;
> to the melody of your harps I will not listen. (5:21-23)

God's denunciation of false worship could have a familiar ring about it in the twenty-first century. In modern parlance, could it be that God would say, "I hate your solemn observances. Even if you give me huge offerings, I will not accept them. I will have no regard for your special offerings. Take away from me the noise of your songs! I will not listen to the music of your pianos, organs, and orchestras"? As horrifying as this bit of invention strikes us, perhaps we need to take a closer look at how sincerely and how spiritually we are trying to please the Lord with our public services.

KEY PRAYER THEME FOR AMOS
Worship Without Justice (5:7,21-27; 7:1-9)[2]

Amos begins with God's punishing a number of nations, including Israel and Judah. He commanded that Israel seek Him in order to live, with an intense announcement of all His powers (5:4-13) and ends with a threatening description of the Day of the Lord (5:20). All this climaxes with the strong denunciation of false worship in the third group of key verses above (5:21-23).

The Lord announced a second locust plague, and Amos petitioned Him to stop in view of the small size of Jacob (7:1-2). God's plumbline will destroy the house of Jereboam II. Later, when Amaziah threatened Amos, Amos rejoined with the certainty of his call to prophesy (7:15). Although he was a herdsman, he was, more importantly, a man of confident prayer. The prophet ended with the hopeful prophecy of the restoration of David, that is, of Judah (9:11-15). At the very last, God certified His own word, "Yahweh your God has spoken" (9:15, HCSB).

KEY PRAYER VERSE AND THEME FOR OBADIAH
Certainty of Edom's Doom (10,21)

Obadiah, Nahum, and Haggai do not contain prayer proper, but they contain revelation about God and His ways and therefore His relationship to His people. In Obadiah, God was speaking to His people about His judgment of Edom. The key verse and key theme are against Edom and reinforce the ancient rule that God will bless those who bless His people, and will curse those who curse them, which relates to prayer.

Saviors shall go up to Mount Zion
to rule Mount Esau,
and the kingdom shall be the LORD's. (verse 21)

KEY PRAYER VERSE FOR JONAH

From inside the specially prepared fish, Jonah prayed,

I called out to the LORD, out of my distress,
and he answered me;
out of the belly of Sheol I cried,
and you heard my voice. (2:2)

KEY PRAYER THEME FOR JONAH

A Prophet's Successful and Unsuccessful Prayer (1:5-6; 2:1-9;
3:5; 4:2-4)

Jonah contains two important prayers. The sailors unsuccessfully
cried to their gods in the storm, but when they discovered the fault
lay with Jonah, they cried to his God for deliverance, and God heard
them (1:14). Jonah's prayer inside the fish was successful (2:1-10).
Jonah's jealously angry prayer after Nineveh's repentance brought a
gentle rebuke from the Lord (4:4). Once again, Jonah prayed an
angry prayer when his sheltering plant withered, but God pointed
out that if Jonah cared about the plant, why shouldn't God care
about Nineveh (4:10-11)?

KEY PRAYER VERSES FOR MICAH

In the book of Micah, the prophet issued a prolonged condemnation
of the sins of Samaria and Jerusalem. However, in the prophetic tra-
dition, Micah ends with a note of hope in one of the two key prayer
verses:

Who is a God like you, pardoning iniquity
and passing over transgression
for the remnant of his inheritance?
He does not retain his anger forever,
because he delights in steadfast love. (7:18)

A second key prayer verse emerges in Micah's message. It concerns an important key to vital prayer:

He has told you, O man, what is good;
and what does the LORD require of you
but to do justice, and to love kindness,
and to walk humbly with your God? (6:8)

KEY PRAYER THEME FOR MICAH
The Pray-er's Alternation of Hope and Despair (3:4,7; 7:7)

Micah began by describing his heartbreak over the sins of the people. He has a particular judgment for unjust leaders (3:1-4). He revealed God's refusal to respond to their prayers:

Then they will cry to the LORD,
but he will not answer them;
he will hide his face from them at that time,
because they have made their deeds evil. (3:4)

Micah had strong condemnation for superstitious workers.

The seers shall be disgraced,
and the diviners put to shame;
they shall all cover their lips,
for there is no answer from God. (3:7)

We saw in Amos a fierce denunciation of the wrong in the people's songs. Now in Micah, the prophet repeated the denunciation by condemning their sacrifices:

> With what shall I come before the LORD,
>> and bow myself before God on high?
>
> Shall I come before him with burnt offerings,
>> with calves a year old?
>
> Will the LORD be pleased with thousands of rams,
>> with ten thousands of rivers of oil?
>
> Shall I give my firstborn for my transgression,
>> the fruit of my body for the sin of my soul? (6:6-7)

The prophets often dwelt on the importance of the spiritual aspect of worship rather than the physical, outward observances that can be "performed" instead of truly offered with a sincere mind and spirit. Micah concluded his book with an answer to his prayer for Judah:

> He will again have compassion on us;
>> he will tread our iniquities underfoot.
>
> You will cast all our sins
>> into the depths of the sea. (7:19)

This follows an exceptional verse (7:18) that shows how thorough God's forgiveness is.

KEY PRAYER VERSE AND THEME FOR NAHUM
God's Protection

Nahum, like Obadiah and Haggai, contains no overt prayer. Nahum demonstrates intimacy sheltering under the rock of the Lord. It builds on what Obadiah had prophesied. The key prayer verse implies a strong relationship with God:

The LORD is good,

> a stronghold in the day of trouble;

he knows those who take refuge in him. (1:7)

God announced His key prayer theme by telling Israel of His protection for those who take refuge in Him and, conversely, His wrath for His enemies through the example of Nineveh. The great city had repented under Jonah, but now, perhaps a hundred or more years later, the people had become cruel and oppressive. The prophet asked, "For upon whom has not come your unceasing evil?" (3:19).

KEY PRAYER VERSES FOR HABAKKUK

Although he heard frightening answers to a series of questions, Habakkuk affirmed an invincible faith:

Though the fig tree should not blossom,

> nor fruit be on the vines,

the produce of the olive fail

> and the fields yield no food,

the flock be cut off from the fold

> and there be no herd in the stalls,

yet I will rejoice in the LORD;

> I will take joy in the God of my salvation.

GOD, the Lord, is my strength;

> he makes my feet like the deer's;

> he makes me tread on my high places. (3:17-19)

May God help us to walk with Him in His high places!

KEY PRAYER THEME FOR HABAKKUK
A Prayer-Struggle Toward Faith (1:1,12-17; 3:1-19)

Habakkuk's first question involved his bewilderment at the wickedness of the nation (1:1-4); he cried to the Lord but God had an unusual "answer" (1:2), which was no comfort. God would punish Judah by using the Chaldeans (1:5-11). God replied to this paradox by informing Habakkuk that the vision would come in God's own time. In the middle of this poem, we have another of those many prophetic declarations that worship must be inward and spiritual: "The righteous shall live by his faith" (2:4), one of the most important statements in the Old Testament, and found again in Romans and James. In a series of five woes, God declared that the earth would be filled with the knowledge of the Lord's glory as water covers the sea (2:14).

In spite of his bafflement, Habakkuk ended his prophecy with one of the most glorious psalms in the Bible (3:2-19). He ended with the words at the beginning of the poem, "He makes my feet like a deer's; he makes me tread on my high places" (3:19; see the key verses at the beginning of the Habakkuk section).

KEY PRAYER VERSE FOR ZEPHANIAH

Zephaniah's description of the Day of the Lord terrifies the reader (1:1-18). After naming his judgment against the nations, God promised restoration:

> At that time I will change the speech of the peoples
> > to a pure speech,
> that all of them may call upon the name of the LORD. (3:9)

Centuries after Enosh, God still will have us "call" on Him!

Key Prayer Theme for Zephaniah
God's Judgment for Not Calling Upon the Lord (1:4-6)

God began this revelation by cutting off those who have served foreign gods (1:4-6). In a demand for repentance, God called on His people to seek Him and to seek humility (2:3). Zephaniah (for God) condemned the various nations for their false gods and pronounced God's sentence on Jerusalem. God's judment was expressed by contrasting the wrath of God against Judah's wickedness with His extraordinary love, surpassing even the condition of His people. Zephaniah's ending proclaims a restoration of the city and the nation. The book ends with God's affirming the prophet's declaration (3:19) and with the declaration that God is speaking (3:20).

Key Prayer Verse and Theme for Haggai
God Must Come First

Haggai also articulates no overt prayer, but in the key verse he strongly urged the Israelites to build the house of the Lord. Remember that the temple was a "house of prayer" (Isaiah 56:7).

> Is it a time for you yourselves to dwell in your paneled houses, while this [God's] house lies in ruins? (1:4)

In his key prayer theme, Haggai established the priorities — God's house must come before the people's houses. The people responded with fear of the Lord (1:12), and Haggai reassured them that God had spoken: "I am with you, declares the LORD" (1:13). The Lord reproved them for defilement, apparently through an unclean offering (2:14) — a constant reminder throughout the prophets that God's work must be done with holy hands. Haggai ended his book with a blessing on the governor, Zerubbabel.

KEY PRAYER VERSE FOR ZECHARIAH

Zechariah recounted many visions but promised that a remnant of one-third of the people would be preserved. God said,

> And I will put this third into the fire,
>> and refine them as one refines silver,
>> and test them as gold is tested.
> They will call upon my name,
>> and I will answer them.
> I will say, "They are my people";
>> and they will say, "The LORD is my God." (13:9)

The last verse is a prophecy of how joyous Israel will be when it returns to the Lord.

KEY PRAYER THEME FOR ZECHARIAH

A Prophet's Apocalyptic Prayer That Envisions the Restoration of God's People (8:4-6,19-22; 13:9)

Zechariah told the returned exiles the message from God: "Return to me, says the LORD of hosts, and I will return to you" (1:3). God expects a reciprocal relationship with us. The initiative comes from God; the obedience comes from us. In the middle of a series of apocalyptic visions, God emphasized once again the spiritual nature of His kingdom, as He had with Isaiah, Amos, Micah, and others. He tells us, "Not by might nor by power, but by my Spirit" (4:6).

God gave eight visions to the prophet, but then spoke about false worship. He repeated Isaiah's restriction on the meaning of a true fast: "When you fasted and mourned in the fifth month and in the seventh, for these seventy years, was it for me that you fasted? And when you eat and when you drink, do you not eat for yourselves and drink for yourselves?" (7:5-6). Referring to their ancestors, God once again emphasized their failed reciprocity: "As I called, and they would not hear, so they called, and I would not hear" (7:13).

Beginning with chapter 8, God gave Zechariah a series of breathtaking visions with awesome promises. Describing the future peace of the city, God asked, "If it is marvelous in the sight of the remnant of this people in those days, should it also be marvelous in my sight?" (8:6). Foreigners would come seeking the Lord's favor (8:21). God had a word about their future prayer:

> Ask rain from the LORD
>> in the season of the spring rain,
> from the LORD who makes the storm clouds,
>> and he will give them showers of rain,
>>> to everyone the vegetation in the field. (10:1)

Perhaps the most exhilarating of all the promises concerned the forgiveness of their past.

> I will bring them back because I have compassion on them,
>> *and they shall be as though I had not rejected them,*
>> for I am the LORD their God and I will answer them.
>> (10:6, emphasis added)

The Lord's crowning promise declared that all things (horses, pots, sacrifices) in Jerusalem would be holy to the Lord (14:20-21). Our little minds cannot take in the splendor of that universal holiness.

KEY PRAYER VERSE FOR MALACHI

Through most of the first chapter, God issued a diatribe against false worship. In the key verse, God expressed His concern with a question:

A son honors his father, and a servant his master. If then I am a father, where is my honor? And if I am a master, where is my fear? says the Lord of hosts to you, O priests, who despise my name. (1:6)

Key Prayer Theme for Malachi
True and False Worship (1:5-9,11-14; 2:11-14)

Unworthy worship fills the last book of the Old Testament. This final book announced unequivocally, "From the rising of the sun to its setting my name will be great among the nations" (1:11). In chapter 2, the people wept because God did not accept their offerings (2:13). God pointed out their hypocrisy by describing His weariness of their insincere questioning about His disapproval. They falsely claimed, "'Everyone who does evil is good in the sight of the Lord, and he delights in them.' Or asked, 'Where is the God of justice?'" (2:17).

God promised a messenger of the covenant who would come in judgment (3:1) and lead a private life with God (which indicates prayer). Another aspect of the people's false worship (worship being a form of prayer) lay in their failure to tithe (3:8-9). God promised a return back to them with interest if they would only pay their due to the Lord.

God announced reward in the Day of the Lord for those who obey Him and burning like a furnace for the wicked (4:1-3). Elijah the prophet would come before the great and awesome Day of the Lord. Some, following this prophet, would restore family values "lest I come and strike the land with a decree of utter destruction" (4:6).

The first book of the Old Testament begins with blessings and curses, and the last Old Testament book follows that same pattern. Prophet after prophet emphasized the spiritual aspect of the law. The centuries after Malachi produced an even greater emphasis on the legal and physical, without regard to the spiritual. The intertestamental literature prepared the way for God to reveal new paths for His people to take in prayer.

Chapter Eleven

MATTHEW, MARK

KEY PRAYER VERSES FOR MATTHEW

Jesus Himself emphasized the key to prayer in His model prayer for all of us:

> Our Father in heaven,
>> hallowed be your name.
>> Your kingdom come,
>> your will be done,
>>> on earth as it is in heaven.
>> Give us this day our daily bread,
>> and forgive us our debts,
>>> as we also have forgiven our debtors.
>> And lead us not into temptation,
>> but deliver us from evil. (6:9-13)

Many volumes have been written about the various nuances of this prayer, which should properly be called the Model Prayer, as Jesus said, "Pray then like this." Each line could be elaborated on extensively, and has been in the many books and dictionaries on the market.

The Model Prayer should become for us an orientation to infinity. Each line concentrates on God—His holiness, fatherhood, name, kingdom, and will. Holiness, or God's glory, is placed first. When God's purposes are accomplished, Jesus has us turn to our earthly concerns—food, forgiveness, and deliverance from temptation or trial. In the first half of the prayer, we concentrate on the spiritual; the second half gives attention to our own needs (but note that only the first petition, for bread, is physical). The entire prayer exhibits a profound reliance on God for all of life—first the spiritual and then the physical.

Reading the Bible Through

I first read the Bible through in 1950 in Hokkaido, Japan. I dutifully started with Genesis and plowed my way through Revelation. When I realized that it was the wise decision of the Holy Trinity to reveal the Godhead through the Incarnation, I realized that to know the Father and the Holy Spirit, I must understand their character through the life of Jesus. I finally located twenty-three harmonies of the gospels and carefully studied, one by one, all of them. I was astonished at the light they shed on the rest of the Bible. My procedure since then has been to read one passage in the Old Testament, one in the Gospels, and one in the letters. I strongly recommend the Navigators system of Scripture memory. Memorizing biblical passages has played a major role in my own development.

KEY PRAYER THEMES FOR MATTHEW
Kingdom Worship (2:11; 4:10; 15:31; 28:9)

Aside from the many aspects of praise praying, most of the prayer of the Old Testament concerns asking in crisis. But the Model Prayer begins by pointing in our need to the Fatherhood. However, most of the prayer in the New Testament centers on praying for the kingdom. This is especially obvious in Jesus' teaching on the Sermon on the Mount (Matthew 5–7).

Significantly, the first three times prayer is mentioned concern worship. The inquiry of the Magi concerned the newborn King of the Jews they had come to worship (2:2). When they found the baby, they fell on their knees and worshipped Him (2:11). God arranged for the opening prayers of the New Testament to emphasize the glory of God; we begin with worship. In the last temptation, Jesus quoted to Satan Deuteronomy 6:13: "You shall worship the Lord your God, and him only shall you serve" (4:10).

During the three recorded temptations, Jesus was fasting (later associated with mourning; 9:14-15). Fasting indicates something of the high regard Jesus had for the tests He was going through (worth a whole chapter, but not pertinent to our present study of prayer). It behooves us to be serious beforehand when we know we are going to face a trial or a test.

Every chapter of the Sermon on the Mount (5–7; "the Kingdom Manifesto") contains some teaching on prayer. Jesus taught more on prayer than any other person in the Bible. In 5:44, He commanded us to love our enemies and pray for those who persecute us. Praying for our enemies reflects the nobility of His nature and of our new character in Christ. Jesus knew of the persecution that lay ahead for Him; the lament in 23:37 tells us that He often wanted to gather Jerusalem's hostile children together "as a hen gathers her brood under her wings."

Chapter 6 begins the first of much formal teaching on prayer. Jesus first told us not to flaunt our prayers as the hypocrites do; they already have their reward in their public display. He tells His followers to pray in secret (6:5-6). Luke emphasized Jesus' practice of much private prayer. Later, after feeding the five thousand, Jesus went up into a mountain to pray alone (14:23), a frequent practice in His prayer life.

Our "closet" may not be a geographical location. Hannah's closet was in the temple as she prayed silently. Nehemiah's secret place was in the presence of the king while his prayer was mute. In both cases, the important reason God heard their prayer was that it was not for display; it was for God and not for man. The lesson for us is that prayer must be in our heart for God. We practice that if we are praying alone.

Jesus also cautions us not to babble (inanity; some translations use "vain repetition") in our prayers. In Elijah's contest, the priests of Baal cried all day long, "Baal, answer us!" (1 Kings 18:26). Elijah mocked their babbling: "Cry aloud, for he is a god. Either he is musing, or he is relieving himself, or he is on a journey, or perhaps he is asleep and must be awakened" (1 Kings 18:27). After Demetrius stirred up a riot against Paul, the crowd shouted for two hours, "Great is Artemis of the Ephesians!" (Acts 19:34).

The Lord wisely chose the word *babble*. That concept of being careful with words in prayer is not to be confused with Jesus' later instructions to persevere in prayer.[1] Perseverance indicates earnestness; these biblical examples of babbling indicate frenzy.[2] These prattlers believed they would be heard for their loud and thoughtless repetition; importunity, on the other hand, demonstrates thoughtfulness. It indicates a devotion to a righteous cause.

After giving us the Model Prayer, the Lord elaborated on the forgiveness called for in it. In forgiving, we are becoming like God, or, if you wish, conforming to the image of Christ. When we confess a sin, God faithfully forgives that problem. God's forgiveness wipes out our sins (Isaiah 43:25); it blots them out (Psalm 51:9), it washes them in the blood of Christ (1 Corinthians 6:11). When God forgives a sin, He forgets it (Isaiah 43:25; Jeremiah 31:34; Hebrews 10:17). Confessing our sin means God obliterates its history in our lives. He annihilates the past!

Herein lies our difficulty: God leaves us in this fleshly world where the father of lies continues to disturb us by reminding us of our forgiven sin. We need not trouble God with more requests for forgiveness; God leaves us in this sinful environment even as He Himself overcame His circumstances common to all of us (Esther 8:17; Jeremiah 15:10; Revelation 2:7,11,17,26; 3:5,12,21). The Revelation passages call the overcomer the "victor."

Jesus next warned about false fasting in the same way He had warned about prayer. We fast for God and His purposes (Isaiah 58); we cannot look for the approval of people. The same promise applies to true fasting that Jesus earlier applied to true prayer — "Your Father who sees in secret will reward you" (6:18).

Kingdom Behavior in Prayer (5:44; 6:5-13; 7:7-11; 18:18-20; 19:13-14; 26:39-44)

The sermon's next reference to prayer (7:7-12) begins with a present progressive imperative: "Ask . . . seek . . . knock." The form of the verb indicates continuous action. Here Jesus emphasized persistence or importunity; He returned to this theme in Luke 11 and 18. This command will be illustrated later in Matthew 15:21-28.

If we "hear" the commands to ask, seek, and knock in the context of the kingdom teaching all through the sermon, we understand that these imperative verbs refer to the entire sermon, especially the command in 6:33: "But seek first the kingdom of God and His righteousness, and all these things will be provided for you" (HCSB). The "but" conjunction in 6:33 refers to all the things previously mentioned that we need not worry about—what to eat, what to drink, and what to wear. The purpose of the sermon is to get us to pray for God's kingdom and His righteousness first, and God will provide those necessities that so many of us concentrate on in our praying. When we pray for the kingdom, God will provide our needs. Even in the Model Prayer, only one petition is for daily bread, not bread for next week.

Jesus then went into great detail about the Father's willingness to answer. He contrasted how an ordinary human father would answer a request from his child with how willingly the Heavenly Father stands ready to grant requests.

> Or which one of you, if his son asks him for bread, will give him a stone? Or if he asks for a fish, will give him a serpent? If you then, who are evil, know how to give good gifts to your children, how much more will your Father who is in heaven give good things to those who ask him! (7:9-11)

Note that Jesus has the human father giving the opposite of what the child requested.

In our human weakness, sometimes we fail to perceive the good gifts that God gives, especially when they don't line up precisely with our request. The Father gives "good gifts." What He gives may be better, or it may be different from what we ask. If we ask for a bicycle, He may give us a car. On the other hand, if God wants to conform us to the image of Christ, He may have a previous program in mind for us that will turn out to be a test (that we would have avoided). If that is the case, the good gift may move us into a higher nobility or generosity than we would have otherwise developed.

Throughout my wife's several cancers, we chose to pray for healing. God chose for us a deeper reliance on Him—through surgery, chemotherapy, radiation, and many other discomforts—that eventually turned out to improve our personal growth in endurance, waiting, and dependence on God. During Laverne's first cancer, God led us to Psalm 16:8, "Because he is at my right hand, I shall not be shaken." Our reliance on God deepened immeasurably during the test. At the end of her chemotherapy, Laverne claimed, "If I had to choose between not having cancer—and not learning these new lessons—or having surgery, nausea, and losing my hair, yet learning this deeper dependence on hourly depending on God through trial, I would choose the cancer with its accompanying new insights." Laverne finally passed away after twenty-seven years of repeated healings, so God answered prayer for a long time.

Our new firmness in faith later took us through other, more difficult trials. During our daughter's year of cancer with six surgeries, eight months of chemotherapy, and six weeks of radiation, the Holy Spirit awakened both my daughter and me early every morning to teach us how to see life through God's perspective. This time it was not a new reliance on God, but rather a larger outlook on God's purposes for life; this happened when life itself became more precious to us. We would share these insights with her children.

In the last month of my daughter's treatment, an American Cancer Society spokesperson began a television commercial with the striking proclamation, "Breast cancer, the disease women fear most!" Our fourteen-year-old granddaughter responded, "Mom, how can he say that? This year of your cancer has been the best thing that ever happened to us!"

Following His instruction on asking, Jesus assured us of God's goodness in His answers by comparing a human father responding to his child's requests by noting for us, "If you then, who are evil, know how to give good gifts to your children, how much more will your Father who is in heaven give good things to those who ask him!" (7:11). Time and again, my family and I have asked one request, only to have God lead us into something greater and better than we could have imagined, greater than our immediate appeal.

After His teaching on prayer, Jesus informed us that prayer itself may be false. Many will claim to have called on Him ("Lord, Lord") and will claim to have done good works in His name. Prayer that God considers valid comes from the person who does the will of Jesus' Father in heaven (7:21-23).

Matthew and all the gospels give us many examples of people appealing to Jesus for healing. Interwoven among all these are constant references to the kingdom. The King was not only a ruler; He was a healer. Among all those examples of healing are listed every kind of disease understood at that time.[3] Most of the healings were at the request of the ill person; some were on behalf of another (9:2,6-8); one woman did not have the courage to ask, only the nerve to touch the hem of Jesus' garment.

Kingdom Faith (and Other Matters) (8:5-13,24-26; 9:20-22; 14:28-32; 15:21-28; 17:17-20; 21:18-22)

A remarkable example of Gentile faith is the Roman centurion's faith that Jesus could heal his servant. Jesus pointed out that He had not found faith like that in Israel. In chapter 15 a touching example of perseverance comes from the Gentile Canaanite woman whom Jesus tested repeatedly before He healed her daughter, probably to exhibit to His disciples the meaning of real faith under pressure. Unique in Jesus' dealings with disease were encounters with faith that could recognize spiritual authority (8:5-13).

Before Jesus healed the paralytic's body, He forgave the sick man's sins. He did this to show that His authority was wide-ranging, from the forgiveness of sins to healing (and to show that spiritual cleansing is more important than physical healing). He demonstrated the same authority when He raised the synagogue official's daughter from the dead. In both instances, Jesus silenced some would-be critics.

He often pointed out the faith of those he healed. He complimented the faith of the centurion asking on behalf of a sick servant (8:10). He told the woman with the issue of blood, "Your faith has made you well" (9:22). He told the two blind men, "According to your faith be it done to you" (9:29). After sternly testing her, Jesus told the Canaanite woman, "O woman, great is your faith! Be it done for you as you desire" (15:28), which indicates that sometimes God wants to give more than we know how to ask; He placed the woman on the roll call of Bible greats. Matthew records that Jesus did not do many miracles in Nazareth because of the people's unbelief (13:58), and as Peter sank in the waves, the Lord chided him, "You of little faith, why did you doubt?" (14:31).

Jesus made an important point with His disciples when He told them that their failure to understand His caution to beware of the leaven of the Pharisees and Sadducees was because of their lack of faith (15:8-11; they were concerned about bread). Our understanding of the spiritual world, as well as the physical, depends on the depth of our faith.

Some of His nature miracles—the feedings of the five thousand and the four thousand, walking on water, and others—were not in answer to prayer. (The calming of the sea, a nature miracle, was in response to the disciples' plea, "Save us, Lord; we are perishing" [8:25]). God often chooses to take the initiative when our requests would probably be either unspiritual or meager.

Jesus refused to give a sign when the Pharisees and Sadducees asked for one; this is a case of a "no" answer (note the wisdom in Jesus' "no" answers to several who wanted to follow Him, in order to keep His own ministry on a right course). The "scholars'" request was insincere, intended to put Jesus in a predicament. He, of course, detected their hypocrisy and pointed out their evil intentions (16:1-4).

Jesus' healing of the demon-possessed boy at the foot of the Mount of Transfiguration teaches that prayer has levels of power. The disciples had tried to rid the boy of the demon, and when Jesus succeeded, He explained that their littleness of faith handicapped them (17:17-20).

In connection with treatment of a sinning brother, the Lord promised that if two are agreed, their prayer will be answered. His statement is rather firm: "If two of you agree on earth about *anything* they ask, it will be done for them by my Father in heaven. For where two or three are gathered in my name, there am I among them" (18:19-20, emphasis added).

Another kingdom lesson lies in Jesus' reaction to the children brought to Him. Some people (parents?) had asked that He touch the children and pray over them. When the disciples rebuked the people bringing them, Jesus made an essential description of the kingdom He had discussed so many times: "Leave the children alone, and don't try to keep them from coming to Me, because the kingdom of heaven is made up of people like this" (19:14, HCSB). (Remember, this is divine authority speaking.)

Jesus did not directly deny the request from the rich young ruler. Jesus told him to sell all his possessions, give them to the poor, and follow him. The rich man went away sorrowing, and yet Jesus had not denied his request. He simply pointed out the failure in the young man's character (19:16-22). Perhaps some of our prayer failures result when we are not forsaking all for the Master.

Another example of unanswered prayer happened when the mother of the sons of Zebedee asked that her sons sit on Jesus' right and left hands in His kingdom. Jesus pointed out that she did not know what she was asking (20:20-22). Could we learn about prayer for ourselves from that rebuke? Only the Father will determine the positions near Jesus in the final kingdom.

The triumphal entry occasioned praise from children (remember that Matthew's recorded prayers started with worship!). When the priests and scribes objected, Jesus told them, "Out of the mouth of infants and nursing babies you have prepared praise" (21:16). Some of our most valuable lessons come from children (18:3).

Jesus seized every opportunity to teach on faith, as in the cursing of the fig tree. When asked about it, Jesus assured them,

> Truly, I say to you, if you have faith and do not doubt, you will not only do what has been done to the fig tree, but even if you say to this mountain, "Be taken up and thrown into the sea," it will happen. And whatever you ask in prayer, you will receive, if you have faith. (21:21-22)

After the famous woes of Matthew 23, Jesus warned His enemies that they would not see Him again until they cry, "Blessed is he who comes in the name of the Lord" (23:39). In the next chapter, after describing great tribulation, He warned again, "Pray that your flight may not be in winter or on a Sabbath" (24:20). Even if we don't understand why, when Jesus commands us to pray in a certain way, we would be foolish not to obey.

In Gethsemane, Jesus cautioned the disciples to stay awake and pray. Matthew carefully recorded their failure. The disciples failed to pray when commanded. Twice in the garden, Jesus begged that the Father might remove the cup from Him but concluded that if it cannot pass, "Your will be done" (26:42). Matthew recorded the last prayer in Matthew, the cry of dereliction, "My God, my God, why have you forsaken me?" (27:46). This prayer seems incomprehensible, but we can be grateful that no believer will ever be forsaken (28:20).

Fittingly, the Great Commission that ends the book begins, "All authority has been given to Me in heaven and on earth" (28:18, HCSB). Repeatedly, Jesus had emphasized His authority in various ways: to forgive sins, to heal disease, and to demand total allegiance. We obey Him because He has "all authority."

KEY PRAYER VERSE FOR MARK

Mark positioned the key prayer verse at the point when the disciples questioned Jesus' assertion that it would be difficult for a rich person (in this case, the rich young ruler) to enter the kingdom of God. He assured them,

> With man it is impossible, but not with God. For all things are possible with God. (10:27)

KEY PRAYER THEME FOR MARK
The Desire of God to Touch His Own Creation (2:4-5,10-12; 5:22-23,35-43; 5:25-34; 7:25-30,31-36; 8:22-25; 9:19-29; 10:13-16,46-52)

John the Baptist used baptism as a sign of repentance, an important kind of prayer to make way for the coming Lord (1:4). As Jesus began His ministry, He also called for repentance (1:15), although He Himself needed no repentance.

Glimpses into the Prayer Life of Jesus

"And rising very early in the morning, while it was still dark, he departed and went out to a desolate place, and there he prayed" (Mark 1:35). "And after he had dismissed the crowds, he went up on the mountain by himself to pray" (Matthew 14:23). "And after he had taken leave of them, he went up on the mountain to pray" (Mark 6:46). "But he would withdraw to desolate places and pray" (Luke 5:16). "Now about eight days after these sayings he took with him Peter and John and James and went up on the mountain to pray" (Luke 9:28).

Mark became the first evangelist to describe Jesus' practice of praying alone: "Rising very early in the morning, while it was still dark, he departed and went out to a desolate place, and there he prayed" (1:35). He must have received the directive to move to other locations in that prayer, because He announced to His disciples when they found Him that they would be moving on to other villages. Later, His attempt to be in a "desolate place" (6:31) was interrupted by one of the many crowds that followed Him and the subsequent feeding of the five thousand. After feeding them, "he went up on the mountain to pray" (6:46).

Jesus gave instructions on fasting in Matthew 6:16-18. However, when John's disciples and the Pharisees asked Him about fasting, He connected it with affliction of the soul (Mark 2:18-20). In Matthew, He had stressed that fasting is a private matter, between the individual and God.

The Old Testament contained miracles, including nature miracles and raising the dead, but healings are not as common as in the New Testament. Yet it would require an encyclopedia to catalog properly the various miracles of Jesus: stilling the storm, feeding multitudes with a minimum amount, knowing the thoughts of people, and many others.

Mark has many healings, besides those mentioned in Matthew.[4] Jesus healed virtually every kind of disease or disorder known in the first century, including many afflictions not included in the Old Testament miracles (the paralytic, blindness, deafness, the crooked back, and others), and He also cast out demons, which do not appear in the Old Testament.

In some cases, the individual asked Jesus directly for healing (1:40, where the man with the skin disease appealed to Jesus' will, which in context assumes God's will; 10:46-52, blind Bartimaeus). In a few instances, others made supplication (2:3-12, the four men lowered the paralytic through the roof in prayer; 7:32-33, a group "begged" Jesus to heal the deaf and mute man).

In feeding the five thousand, Jesus "blessed" the food (6:41). Before feeding the four thousand, He gave thanks (8:6), so blessing a meal and expressing thanks closely amount to the same thing. Even today, we use both expressions for the same act. Matthew (14:19) and Luke (9:16) use the word *blessing* with the feeding of the five thousand. Matthew uses *thanks* with the four thousand (15:36) and John says that Jesus gave thanks in feeding the five thousand (6:11). The terms are equivalent.

Mark also provides examples where Jesus' answer was "no." After Jesus cast out the demons in the Gerasene demoniac, the healed man begged to go with Jesus, and Jesus refused to allow it. This particular refusal occurred several times. Another refusal happened when the Pharisees demanded a sign (8:11-12). On this occasion, their superstition caused Jesus to "[sigh] deeply in his spirit."

An answered prayer comes when, after the Transfiguration, the disciples asked why Elijah had to precede the coming of Jesus. Jesus assured them that Elijah had come (in the person of John the Baptist).

When the disciples were unable to cast a demon out of a boy at the foot of the Mount of Transfiguration, Jesus immediately cast out the demon and the bewildered disciples asked why they could not cast it out. After all, they had cast out demons when Jesus sent them over Galilee (6:13). Jesus told them that this kind of demon came out only by prayer (9:29). As we shall see in Luke, the disciples were aware that even their designated authority did not have the authority of the prayer of Jesus.

The Lord gave the disciples a tender answer when they tried to prevent some people from bringing children to Jesus. Jesus indignantly told the disciples that the kingdom of God belonged "to such" as these (10:14). Jesus was showing the dimensions of prayer. It may be as lowly as children or as lofty as the temple. The temple was to be a house of prayer for all nations or for all people. Jesus' high evaluation of prayer came when He drove the money changers from the temple. On that occasion, Jesus called the temple a "house of prayer" (11:17; quoting Isaiah 56:7). God's house was for God, not for thieves.

Prayer is for God's sake alone; Jesus sternly denounced prayers done for self-exaltation. In His denunciation of the scribes, Jesus sternly warned that they "devour widow's houses and for a pretense make long prayers" (12:40). He was not limiting the length of prayers we may say, but the motive behind them. His own prayer in John 17 was rather long, but the only human hearers were the eleven disciples.

In describing the "great tribulation," Jesus instructed His disciples to pray that their escape (or our escape) "may not happen in winter" (13:18). The preceding part of this discourse encouraged the believers who would go through the Tribulation to flee without regard to the circumstances around them.

In His institution of the Lord's Supper, or Communion, Jesus once again expressed thanks, as He had done with the mass feedings. Most sincere believers through the centuries have followed Jesus' example with this pattern.

The famous Gethsemane prayers (14:32-42) are often cited as an example of Jesus' humanness. Rather, they reflect the extremity of suffering (not just physical, but sin-bearing and separation from His Father) He was about to undergo. He wanted to be strengthened by the prayers of nearby disciples, but they failed Him. All believers can learn from His warning to the sleeping disciples: "Stay awake and pray so that you won't enter into temptation. The spirit is willing, but the flesh is weak" (14:38, HCSB). Jesus had to face the tortures ahead utterly alone. This tells us how urgent it is that we pray for those near us who are suffering. The work of Calvary is a greater work and a greater accomplishment than the creation of the universe or the creation of man and woman. Jesus was left to complete the titanic work of redemption totally alone.

Experts have written volumes about Jesus' mysterious cry of desolation, "My God, my God, why have you forsaken me?" (15:34). Inherent in that cry is the enormity of the work He was accomplishing. All we who come after can do is to reverently bow to the greatest work of all time, and to the Man who carried it through to an end far more comprehensive than anyone can imagine.

Chapter Twelve

LUKE

KEY PRAYER VERSES FOR LUKE

The key prayer verses for Luke emphasize perseverance:

> I tell you, ask, and it will be given to you; seek, and you will find;
> knock, and it will be opened to you. (11:9-10)

Jesus' commands to pray must be within the outlook of the godly prayers in this book. James and John *asked* selfishly for high positions. Saul *sought* to retain his throne. The asking command and the seeking command are contained within instruction for the kingdom.

KEY PRAYER THEMES FOR LUKE

Luke provides more information on prayer than any other gospel. Not only does it include more prayers than most of the other books, but it also contains more teaching on prayer, all by Jesus. The richness of prayer in Luke demands two themes to cover all of it.

Jesus Modeling Prayer (3:21; 5:16; 6:12; 9:18,28; 10:21-22; 11:1; 22:32; 23:34)

Significantly, when Gabriel announced the coming of Jesus' forerunner to Zechariah, "the whole multitude of the people were praying outside [the temple] at the hour of incense" (1:10). Prayer characterizes the story of Jesus from His forerunner to His ascension. The angel told Zechariah, "Do not be afraid, Zechariah, for your prayer has been heard" (1:13). Either Zechariah and Elizabeth had prayed for a child in their youth, or else they had persisted for years in that prayer. The context, with Zechariah's disbelief, indicates that for some time the couple had given up on that prayer. Gabriel's phrase, however, indicates that they had not forgotten their years of praying for a child.

Mary's prayer in Elizabeth's home (1:46-55) locks in a theme that will dominate much of Jesus' later teaching: God will reverse many factors of earthly importance (the rich will become poor; the mourners will laugh). Mary said that God scatters the proud because of the thoughts of their hearts, topples the mighty from their thrones and exalts the lowly, satisfies the hungry with good things and sends the rich away empty (1:51-53). The poem expresses praise, beginning with God's greatness and rejoicing in Him as her savior; it ends with God's mercy to Israel.

After the Baptist's birth, God loosened Zechariah's frozen tongue in praise (1:64). In his prayer, the priest first spoke of redemption and salvation (1:68-71), of deliverance from their enemies (1:74), then of John's future role (1:76) and of the great sequel to John's ministry (1:77-79). Both Mary's "Magnificat" and Zechariah's "Benedictus" are masterpieces of poetry that have been memorized countless times in praise of God. The acts of God and the names of God described in these prayers still furnish Christians with praise-evoking names and attributes of the Lord.

When the angels announced Jesus' birth to the shepherds, the angels began with "Glory to God in the highest" (2:14). What would a dimensional term like *highest* mean to pure spirits? Obviously the heavenly announcers had to use terms that signified cosmic beyondness for the sake of their earthbound hearers, and even today we can scarcely take in more than those herdsmen. (Any distance from earth would be "highest" regardless of its direction from earth.) With the light in the sky, the shepherds must have been terrified (2:9). The angels announced that God's peace was for "those with whom he is pleased" (2:14). After seeing the newborn Lord, the shepherds returned, glorifying and praising God (2:20). It must have been a spectacular experience, long to be remembered (who told Luke this story?).

Joseph and Mary dutifully presented the new baby in their sacrifice in the temple; Simeon, a Spirit-filled man, was supernaturally enabled to recognize the significance of this child and composed a beautiful paean of thanksgiving. He had been promised that he would see "the consolation of Israel" (2:25). The widow Anna, whose lifetime had been devoted to fastings and prayers, echoed Simeon's insights with thanksgiving (2:36-38). Only Luke records the many poems spanning the expanse of the birth narrative. A stunning prayer in the form of a hymn accompanies every major turn of the story.

Jesus and the Holy Spirit

"Jesus, full of the Holy Spirit, returned from the Jordan and was led by the Spirit in the wilderness for forty days" (Luke 4:1-2). "But if it is by the Spirit of God that I cast out demons, then the kingdom of God has come upon you" (Matthew 12:28). "And everyone who speaks a word against the Son of Man will be forgiven, but the one who blasphemes against the Holy Spirit will not be forgiven" (Luke 12:10).

In Luke, each major event occurred when Jesus had prayed, or was in prayer. At His baptism, the Holy Spirit descended when He "was praying" (3:21), and God affirmed Him with a voice from heaven. After His baptism, the Spirit continued His spiritual ministry and led Jesus into the wilderness (4:1) for a series of temptations to fulfill His royal destiny with worldly shortcuts (4:3-12).

Luke also records many miracles and healings.[1] Among miracles not yet mentioned are the healing of Simon's mother-in-law (4:38-39), the raising of the son of the widow of Nain (7:15, which caused all the townspeople to glorify God), and the ten leprous men (17:12-19). The latter incorporated an object lesson of the Samaritan alone returning to thank Jesus. Luke frequently emphasized that Jesus healed all who were sick with various diseases (4:40; 6:18; 7:21).

Luke, more than any other evangelist, repeatedly returned to the theme of Jesus praying alone. Luke also referred to the interruptions that quelled those attempts (4:42). In 5:16, "he would withdraw to desolate places and pray." The night before He chose the twelve apostles, he prayed on a mountain all night (6:12-13). While he was praying alone His disciples asked Him to teach them how to pray. At His transfiguration, only Peter, James, and John were present to see Him praying as the momentous kingdom manifestation occurred.

Jesus was praying when every major event of his life happened — at His baptism, in healing, in choosing the Twelve, at His transfiguration, and, of course, in Gethsemane, and on the cross. He prayed for Simon before Simon's betrayal (22:32).

Jesus' Teaching on Prayer

Jesus taught more on prayer than any other person in the Bible. That in itself should make obvious God's view of the importance of prayer. Jesus not only taught on prayer; He *modeled* it.

His teaching on fasting in Mark 2 is repeated in Luke 5:33-35. The spirit of the Sermon on the Mount is reiterated in 6:28: "Bless those who curse you, and pray for those who abuse you." This is one of Jesus' most difficult teachings, but He fulfilled it by example in 23:34. Praying for our enemies is a sign of high nobility that few believers realize. All Jesus' relationships exhibit an inherent dignity.

Jesus enforced His strong and repeated emphasis on faith in His healings. He complimented the faith of the centurion in 7:9 (see also Matthew 8:10), and that of the woman with the issue of blood (Luke 8:48 and Matthew 9:22). He told the Canaanite woman, "Great is your faith" (Matthew 15:28). He chided the disciples in the storm because of their lack of faith (8:25) and questioned Peter as he sank in the waves, "O you of little faith, why did you doubt?" (Matthew 14:31). In comparing how God clothes the fields with grass, Jesus reiterated, "How much more will he clothe you, O you of little faith!" (12:28).

It seems likely that the disciples failed to cast out the demon at the foot of the Mount of Transfiguration because of their lack of faith. Jesus' words were, "O faithless and twisted generation" (9:41). He assured the blind man near Jericho, "Your faith has made you well" (18:42). He felt that His actions and words should have assured His followers, yet in the parable of the persistent widow, He concluded, "Nevertheless, when the Son of Man comes, will he find faith on earth?" (18:8).

When the disciples asked Jesus to increase their faith, He said, "If you had faith like a grain of mustard seed, you could say to this mulberry tree, 'Be uprooted and planted in the sea,' and it would obey you" (17:6). This may have been the fig tree Jesus cursed in Mark 11:12-14,20-21. On that occasion, Jesus promised, "Truly, I say to you, whoever says to this mountain, 'Be taken up and thrown into the sea,' and does not doubt in his heart, but believes that what he says will come to pass, it will be done for him" (Mark 11:23).

This is followed by an admonition that we are not to pray with an unforgiving heart, as emphasized in the Sermon on the Mount in Matthew 6:14-15.

Jesus' command to ask, seek, and knock primarily concerned praying for kingdom purposes. The command was given as part of the ending of the Sermon on the Mount (Matthew 7:7), but the parallel passage here occurs in the middle of instruction on prayer (11:9; see below), not in the Sermon on the Mount. Luke scattered Jesus' teaching on prayer throughout his gospel. Jesus reinforced this command in 10:2: "The harvest is plentiful, but the laborers are few. Therefore pray earnestly to the Lord of the harvest to send out laborers into his harvest." He followed this by instructing the seventy as He sent them to proclaim the kingdom. On their return, Jesus praised God: "I thank you, Father, Lord of heaven and earth, that you have hidden these things from the wise and understanding and revealed them to little children" (10:21).[2]

Jesus Himself did not choose "the wise and understanding" but fishermen, tax collectors, and prostitutes. Mary's "Magnificat" had spoken of God reversing expected circumstances.

Watching Jesus pray, His disciples asked Him to teach them to pray. He again cited the Model Prayer and supplied this time two parables on persistence, the first about the persistent man who knocked on his neighbor's door until the unwilling neighbor got up and yielded to the man's relentless demands. After this parable, Jesus insisted, "And I tell you, ask, and it will be given to you; seek, and you will find; knock, and it will be opened to you. For everyone who asks receives, and the one who seeks finds, and to the one who knocks it will be opened" (11:9-10). He then repeated the promise, using the parable of a generous father. These hyperboles must have made a profound impression on the disciples, as they should on us. The teaching on persistence related closely to Jesus' command to abide in Him.

Another unanswered prayer occurred when a man asked Jesus to divide His family inheritance. Jesus' answer seems almost brusque, in keeping with His determination to stick to His purpose in the Incarnation. He informed the man that this was not His calling, and warned about "all covetousness" (12:14-15).

Jesus presented an eschatological prayer after His lament over Jerusalem. He warned His listeners, "And I tell you, you will not see

me until you say, 'Blessed is he who comes in the name of the Lord!'"
(13:35). Jesus also demonstrated an unanswered prayer in His parable about the rich man and Lazarus. When the rich man begged
Abraham to send Lazarus to cool his tongue, Abraham reminded the
rich man that a great chasm now separated Lazarus from him.
Abraham also refused to allow Lazarus to go and warn the rich man's
brothers, informing us that if the brothers would not hear Moses and
the prophets, they would not hear one returned from the dead
(16:19-31).

The lesson on the healing of the ten lepers is a lesson on thankfulness. Of all those healed, only a Samaritan returned to thank the
Lord. Compare this ironic twist with Jesus' satisfaction with the
faith of the Gentile centurion and that of the Gentile Canaanite
woman.

In Luke 18, Jesus once again returned to His extensive teaching
on prayer. Luke introduces these new concepts: "And he told them
a parable to the effect that they ought always to pray and not lose
heart" (18:1). Again Jesus used hyperbole; He had talked about
how much more willing God is to give by comparing Him to
unlikely fathers. A widow approached an unjust judge and persis-
tently begged for justice. Jesus concluded, "And will not God give
justice to his elect, who cry to him day and night? Will he delay long
over them? I tell you, he will give justice to them speedily"
(18:7-8).

The Lord then related the story of the bragging Pharisee thankful for his superiority and the lowly tax collector who humbly begged
for mercy (18:9-14). In the Sermon on the Mount, Jesus had denounced
pray-ers who prayed as an exhibition (remember the warning about
false prayers in Matthew 7 ["Lord, Lord"]) and exhorted His followers to pray in a private room (Matthew 6:5-6). Later He would say
that the scribes "for a pretense make long prayers" (20:47). Jesus had
commended several persons on their faith. In the Triumphal Entry,
He accepted the praise of those on the route who were praising him

"with a loud voice" (19:37). When the Pharisees objected, Jesus told them, "I tell you, if these were silent, the very stones would cry out" (19:37-40).

Speaking of the approaching judgment on Jerusalem, Jesus instructed His disciples, "But stay awake at all times, praying that you may have strength to escape all these things that are going to take place, and to stand before the Son of Man" (21:36). Having often emphasized the unexpectedness of His return, He highlighted this command to pray at all times.

A tender prayer that the Lord answered mightily shows Jesus praying for Simon after He had warned Simon that he would fail (22:32). This is an example of the advocacy Jesus is exercising on behalf of His followers even now (1 John 2:1).

Arriving at Gethsemane, Jesus sternly warned His disciples, "Pray that you may not enter into temptation" (22:40). Only He knew the danger their spiritual stance would face in the next hours. Later, when He found them sleeping, He tried again: "Why are you sleeping? Rise and pray that you may not enter into temptation" (22:46). Perhaps if they had stayed awake and prayed, it might have eased the enormity of the burden He was bearing in His own prayer. Their own breakdown that night originated in their failure to pray. We cannot grasp the magnitude of the consequences of our prayerlessness.

Jesus' famous prayer begins "if you are willing." Facing the most cosmic work of all time, He inevitably prayed to be delivered from the horror facing Him, with the caveat, "Nevertheless, not my will, but yours, be done" (22:42). Jesus was carrying out what His disciples failed to carry out—He was praying.

His last prayer was certainly answered: "Father, into your hands I commit my spirit" (23:46). The loud volume of His prayer indicates that He still had reserve strength left. Enormous strength, the result of His prayers, carried Him through the entire ordeal. Prayer was

Jesus' life from first to last. Small wonder that His teaching is the most powerful teaching in the Bible on prayer!

After the Ascension, the disciples worshipped Jesus before returning to Jerusalem. They remained in the temple complex, continually blessing God (24:52-53).

Chapter Thirteen

JOHN

KEY PRAYER VERSES FOR JOHN

The name of Jesus provides a powerful thrust to our prayers. Note in our key prayer verse that prayer completes our joy.

> Truly, truly, I say to you, whatever you ask of the Father in my name,
> he will give it to you. Until now you have asked nothing in my name.
> Ask, and you will receive, that your joy may be full. (16:23-24)

KEY PRAYER THEME FOR JOHN

Asking in Jesus' Name (15:16; 16:23-24,26-27)

A strange curiosity about prayer is that until John 4, the Bible contains no specific teaching as such about worship and praise, and yet the Bible contains more prayer dedicated to worship and praise than any other topic. The great creed of Israel, the Shema, commanded love (which is worship) of God above all else (Deuteronomy 6:5).

Worship and praise relate to one another closely, but we may draw a fine line of distinction between them: worship concerns loving or adoring God while praise is elevating His attributes or His actions. Many, but not all, of the psalms combine both ideas.

The first real instruction in worship comes from the Lord Himself. Jesus told the woman at the well, "God is spirit, and those who worship him must worship in spirit and truth" (4:24). Jesus was, first of all, negating the idea that worship depends on a place—the Samaritan or the Judean temple. Worship in spirit, as nebulous as the concept seems to be, can be understood by contrasting it with its opposites: on the one hand, formulaic worship or worship for exhibition of self (pride, self-consciousness, performance, and so forth); on the other hand, the opposite lies in the attention of the pray-er (on the audience, on private fulfillment of "duty," or on God). We can be assured that it is truly our spirit praying when our worship is neither ritual nor performance. Worship in spirit happens when *all the attention is directed to God.*

We can look at worship in truth more easily. The pray-er must be sincere; God hates a hypocritical prayer. Worship in truth comes from the bottom of our heart. When we make our interest to be God's interest, rather than concentrating on self, we are worshipping in truth. Our preparation for worship, private or public, should give attention to our spirit rather than our dress or on any of the accoutrements our churches have—fine preachers, good music, or even the building. If all our attention is concentrated on God, we are approaching spiritual worship, which, in turn, depends on God's Spirit leading us.

John does not concentrate on healing. Rather, in proving Jesus to be the Christ, the Son of God, John provides a number of signs that vindicate Jesus' deity. Most Bible dictionaries cite seven miracles as the signs of Jesus' diety. However, John names a number of other "minor" miracles that are not usually included in the signs.

In the first minor miracle, the Holy Spirit descended on Jesus at His baptism (1:32-34). The Synoptic Gospels record God speaking to Jesus from heaven (prayer because it is speech from above). A second minor miracle happened when Jesus knew the thoughts of Nathanael (1:47-49). Such a demonstration of prescience brought Nathanael to faith and undoubtedly opened the eyes of Philip, who had already acknowledged Jesus' authority. Jesus manifested a third "minor" miracle in His awareness of the life story of the woman at the well (4:16-26). This miracle brought the village of Sychar to the "Savior of the world" (4:39-42).

The first of the seven signs occurred when Jesus turned the water into wine in Cana (2:3-11). John records that on this occasion, "He displayed His glory, and His disciples believed in Him" (2:11, HCSB).

Prayer entered into the second sign. A royal official in Capernaum begged Jesus to heal his dying son. Jesus tested his faith when He told him, "Unless you [people] see signs and wonders you will not believe" (4:48). The official proved his faith by his persistence, like the centurion in Matthew 8 and the Canaanite woman in Matthew 15. One of the characteristics of Jesus working with His various petitioners was to bring them to persistence, a sign of faith. He used many means to accomplish His various healings: touching, speaking, bringing the woman with the issue of blood out into the open, and even healing in stages. He accomplished the healing of the official's son across distance (4:46-54).

For His third sign, Jesus healed the sick man at the pool of Bethesda. This is one instance where Jesus Himself took the initiative as He watched the pathetic crowd superstitiously waiting for the moving of the water (supposedly by an angel). Jesus approached the man, saying, "Do you want to get well?" (5:6, HCSB). Healing him, Jesus instructed him to take up his bed and walk. Since it was a Sabbath, this occasioned Jewish criticism of breaking the Sabbath. The criticism gave Jesus an opportunity for the first of many discourses[1] in which He plainly laid out His relation to His Father.

In the fourth sign, the feeding of the five thousand, Jesus again took the initiative. When the crowd wanted to make Him king, "He withdrew again to the mountain by Himself" (6:15, HCSB). Repeatedly, individuals or crowds wanted to make Jesus a political king or Messiah, and He had to take strong measures to correct their misunderstanding. He would tell some of those healed, "Tell no man," or He would (miraculously?) walk away from their attention. This happened even when people were hostile (Luke 4:30). He also often had to caution demons not to make Him known (Luke 4:41).

In the fifth sign, Jesus walked on water. Interestingly, only the disciples observed this miracle. Jesus demonstrated His authority over nature when He stilled the storm, walked on water, and ascended into heaven.

An often unnoticed answer to prayer followed His declaration that He came down from heaven as the bread of life. The crowd begged, "Sir, give us this bread always!" That request followed the feeding of the five thousand, and occasioned the famous discourse on the bread of life (6:32-51; Jesus was giving Himself as an answer to that prayer). That difficult discourse also brought about the desertion of many of His dissatisfied followers (6:60-66).

Jesus asked the Twelve if they would likewise desert. Simon Peter answered "Lord, who will we go to? You have the words of eternal life." Jesus answered, but His reply was somewhat oblique: "Didn't I choose you, the Twelve? Yet one of you is the Devil" (6:66-71, HCSB).

He healed the man born blind as His sixth sign. In this case, Jesus placed His saliva mixed with mud on the man's eyes and told the man to wash in the pool of Siloam. Since the healing happened on a Sabbath, the Pharisees questioned the no-longer-blind man, who gave the wise answer, "We know that God does not listen to sinners, but if anyone is a worshiper of God and does His will, God listens to him" (9:31). The healed man, after his interchange with the Pharisees, became a follower of Jesus. When Jesus accused the Pharisees of blindness, it occasioned another of His discourses following a sign, the discourse centering on the good shepherd. The frequency of these discourses after a miracle has caused theologians to call the miracles a "sign."

The Love of God

An unexpected anomaly of the love of God expresses itself in what might be called degrees of love. Size can mean nothing to infinity, just as time can mean nothing to eternity. God loves all people. However, within that incomprehensible infinity, Scripture mentions a special love Jesus had for Lazarus (John 11:3) and for John (John 21:7). Evidently the Bible reveals that God cannot have "size" but He can express His attributes in intimacy.

In the most spectacular sign, the seventh, Jesus raised Lazarus from the dead. Note that Jesus waited until Lazarus had been dead four days before going to Bethany to see him. Jesus' hesitation may be due to two factors. Most importantly, this death was for "the glory of God." The will of God was paramount to Jesus (and to effective pray-ers today). Secondly, by now putrefaction would have set in. Martha said, "Lord, by this time there will be an odor, for he has been dead four days" (11:39). Resuscitation after this length of time would have been more remarkable and unquestionable than the raising of the son of the widow of Nain. Jesus reassured Martha, "Did I not I tell you that if you believed you would see the glory of God?" (11:40). Jesus always centered His actions and word on the glory of God. He would make this unmistakably clear in the Last Discourse.

This sign or wonder, as it became known, inevitably led to much speculation on the part of the populace.[2] The chief priests and the Pharisees convened a meeting of the Sanhedrin over this unquestionable display of divine authority, and they determined that Jesus should die. Later, they decided even to kill Lazarus (11:45-57; 12:9-11).

When Mary anointed Jesus' feet (we may assume in an unspoken prayer of adoration), He spoke of His burial when Judas complained about the "waste": "Leave her alone; she has kept it for the day of My burial. For you always have the poor with you [Judas's complaint], but you do not always have Me" (12:7-8, HCSB).

God is eternal, beyond time, but He has always had a plan for time. Later Paul would say, "For while we were still weak, *at the right time* Christ died for the ungodly" (Romans 5:6, emphasis added). A subsequent notation tells us, "But when the *fullness of time* had come, God sent forth his Son, born of woman, born under the law, to redeem those who were under the law" (Galatians 4:4-5, emphasis added).

This sensitivity to time began before Jesus was born. As John the Baptist began his ministry, he announced, "The time is fulfilled" (Mark 1:15). Even approaching the Feast of Tabernacles, Jesus was sensitive to the time of His going to the feast, as opposed to His brothers (7:6-8). As Jesus approached His fateful last Passover, He said, "My time is at hand" (Matthew 26:18). When Judas left the Passover meal, Jesus announced, "Now is the Son of Man glorified, and God is glorified in him" (13:31). Jesus lived a lifetime conscious of the timing of His Father.

When the Greeks came to Him, He cried, "Now My soul is troubled. What should I say [what prayer?] — Father, save me from this hour? But this is why I came to this hour. Father, glorify your name!" (12:27-28, HCSB).

Note the prayer Jesus did *not* pray. He did not pray for deliverance from Calvary, His destiny. That is the Gethsemane prayer, prayed prior to the last Passover.

The fickleness of the Jerusalem crowd showed itself vividly in the praise they gave to Jesus in the Triumphal Entry: "Hosanna! Blessed is he who comes in the name of the Lord, even the King of Israel [again misunderstanding]!" (12:13).

At the beginning of the Last Discourse,[3] Jesus promised the disciples, "I assure you: The one who believes in Me [faith again] . . .

will do even greater works than these, because I am going to the Father" (14:12, HCSB). Obviously, they could not do a greater work than redemption, a divine work, because they were not divine. But Jesus had spent three and a half years proclaiming the kingdom in His discourses and works. He was the King incarnate in His human role.

Jesus evangelized only a tiny strip of land, Israel, and left in the hands of His disciples the spread of the kingdom. The apostles evangelized the entire north African coast, the entire European coast, the Mediterranean islands, and most of the known Middle East. To Jesus, this spreading of the kingdom was the basic work He came to do, and in this discourse, He entrusted the establishment of the New Testament church and consequent spreading of the kingdom into their hands. That was to be a human-divine work, like what He had done, by the apostles working with the Spirit to enable them.

So what did Jesus say after announcing His departure? Every chapter in the Last Discourse contains material on prayer. He was informing them that they could not spread the kingdom on their own, but must depend on prayer and the coming Helper.

In 14:13-14, He promised, "Whatever you ask in My name, I will do it so that the Father may be glorified in the Son. If you ask Me anything in My name, I will do it" (HCSB). In other words, the disciples could not rely on their own resources; they must rely on God through prayer.

Then in 14:16, He asserted, "And I will ask the Father, and he will give you another [*allon*—another of the same kind] Helper, to be with you forever." This was Jesus' first promise of the coming Holy Spirit, whom He called the "Spirit of truth" (14:17). Jesus promised that the Holy Spirit would "teach you all things"; one of Jesus' primary works was teaching. He told them that the Spirit would "bring to your remembrance all that I have said to you" (14:26), a mammoth task. He assured them that of all His monumental teaching, nothing would be lost.

In 15:7, after the command to remain in Him, He affirmed that that "if you abide in me, and my words abide in you, ask whatever you wish, and it will be done for you." The teaching on abiding or remaining reminds us of the importance of persistence. Then in 15:16 He assured them that the initiative did not lie with them: "You did not choose me, but I chose you and appointed you that you should go and bear fruit and that your fruit should abide, so that *whatever you ask the Father in my name* [not in their merits or their work, but in His character], *he may give it to you*" (emphasis added).

Jesus reminded them that they had much yet to learn: "I still have many things to say to you, but you cannot bear them now" (16:12). He then disclosed the stunning truth that what they would yet learn would come from the Holy Spirit.

> When the Spirit of truth comes, he will guide you into all the truth, for he will not speak on his own authority, but whatever he hears he will speak, and he will declare to you the things that are to come. He will glorify me, for he will take what is mine and declare it to you. All that the Father has is mine; therefore I said that he will take what is mine and declare it to you. (16:13-15)

In the same last chapter of the discourse, He elaborated on all He had been saying:

> In that day you will ask nothing of me. Truly, truly, I say to you, whatever you ask of the Father in my name, he will give it to you. Until now you have asked nothing in my name. Ask, and you will receive, that your joy may be full. (16:23-24)

Two verses later He reinforced His words:

> In that day you will ask in my name, and I do not say to you that I will ask the Father on your behalf; for the Father himself loves you,

because you have loved me and have believed that I came from God. (16:26-27)

In the book of Acts, we shall see how well they understood and obeyed His instruction.

No other Bible prayer approaches the importance of Jesus' prayer in John 17. He began by acknowledging, "Father, the hour has come" (note the "hour" again). The first five verses of this monumental prayer concern redemption, stating that the glory moment had arrived and that eternal life is knowing God. Jesus prayed that those hearing Him would know how He glorified the Father and completed the work assigned to Him from all eternity. They would know God through what Jesus had done and was about to do. The ending of the first section refers to Jesus' existence before all creation. He was the Deity the apostles had gradually come to recognize.

Significantly, the first part of the intercession in this prayer refers to the origin of all Jesus' words and works: the Father. Jesus revealed the name of the Father and acknowledged that the Twelve were a gift from Him. The Father would finish what He initiated. Jesus reminded the Father that the disciples believed the Father's words through Him. He carefully observed that He was not praying for the world, but for His own (17:6-9).

Jesus prayed for the Father to protect and guard them. Then, in an aside, He acknowledged that in returning to His original, eternal home, He had guarded His own in His Incarnation and He said this for them to hear "that they may have My joy completed in them" (17:13, HCSB). He carefully enunciated once more that He was not asking the Father to take them out of the world but to protect them from the Evil One (17:15-16).

In the next three verses, Jesus prayed for their sanctification (17:17-19). He stated that as He was sent into the world, He also has sent them into the world. Our holiness mirrors His sanctity (17:19).

The Lord then prayed, "I pray not only for these, but also for those who believe in Me through their message" (17:20, HCSB). All of us have the same protection and Spirit that His listeners had. At this point, Jesus began a series of prayers for the unity of the believers (17:21-23), like the unity He enjoyed with the Father. Jesus concluded by praying for our future, that we may join Him where He is and see His glory. He reminded the Father that although the world did not know Him, the disciples (and all of us who truly know Him) recognized and believed in all He had said and done.

The magnitude of this prayer consists not only in its incomparable and timeless contents but also in the unmatched nobility of the person who prayed it. Only Jesus could pray these requests, and only the Father could and would hear them because of their Source. We rest safely in His everlasting arms.

All four gospels detail the indescribable horror of the crucifixion. John alone provides the magnificent culmination of this lifetime of incomparable work. After commending His spirit to the Father, Jesus made the grandest announcement ever made: "It is finished" (19:30). Then He bowed His head. In His last act, Jesus prayed.

In the last actual prayer in John, Thomas reluctantly yet enthusiastically acknowledged that the resurrection he had denied for a week was real after all. When he saw Jesus, Jesus even had to confront him with the wounds in His side, hands, and feet. Thomas then cried, "My Lord and my God!" (20:28). This confession ties the whole chapter together. It summarily answers the great prayer of John 17.

Chapter Fourteen

ACTS

KEY PRAYER VERSE FOR ACTS

The key prayer verse for Acts unlocks all the remarkable achievements recorded in this book.

> And they devoted themselves to the apostles' teaching and the fellowship, to the breaking of bread and the prayers. (2:42)

KEY PRAYER THEME FOR ACTS

Progress of the Church Through Prayer (1:14; 2:42,46-47; 6:6; 8:15; 10:1-4,9,30-33; 12:5,12; 13:2-3; 14:23; 16:25; 20:36; 21:5)

At the end of His forty days of post-resurrection appearances, Jesus instructed His followers to wait on the coming of the Holy Spirit (1:4). Once again, not comprehending all He had in mind, they asked if He would restore the kingdom to Israel. Commanding them to wait in Jerusalem for the Father's promise, Jesus replied what we all need to recognize, "It is not for you to know times or seasons that the Father has fixed by his own authority" (1:7). He informed them that the Spirit would enable their witness in Jerusalem, Samaria, and to the ends of the earth.

God gave us a difficult command in His mandate to wait. Waiting (in line, driving down the road) engenders suspense. Suspense usually paralyzes appropriate action, so we need to learn why waiting accomplishes God's purposes. The disciples always obeyed explicitly whatever Jesus commanded, sometimes in a surprising way.

To their credit, not knowing what He had in store for them, the disciples simply waited. Luke tells us that they also obeyed Jesus' commands in the Last Discourse: "All these with one accord were devoting themselves to prayer [remember the command to abide in Him], together with the women and Mary the mother of Jesus, and his brothers" (1:14). Apparently Jesus' brothers had come to faith in the forty-day interim. First Corinthians 15:7 tells us that Jesus appeared to James, so now possibly all the brothers were included in the group, and they were praying. Peter led in the move to replace Judas. In prayer (1:24) they chose Matthias to join them.

Prayer Is Action

Jesus, more than any other individual in the Bible, had given abundant instructions in prayer. The book of Acts shows His instructions being carried out all across the Mediterranean world.

Their waiting prayer led to the prodigious outpouring at Pentecost, when three thousand souls were powerfully added to their number. "They received their food with glad and generous hearts, praising God and having favor with all the people. And the Lord added to their number day by day those who were being saved" (2:46-47).

Significantly, the lame man at the Beautiful Gate of the temple was healed when Peter and John were going to the temple at the hour of prayer (3:1-8). Actually a double miracle happened: the man's lameness was healed, and God instilled into his brain the ability to walk and leap. Today, a recovering cripple must be retrained to walk again. This cripple even "leaped up."

The crowd knew about the disabled man's long begging at the temple; when they saw his new agility, they began praising God for the astonishing miracle (3:9). Peter followed his Master's example—he followed the miracle by a discourse. He announced that God had "glorified his servant Jesus," and emphasized that faith in Jesus' name had accomplished the miracle (3:13-16). Although this speech occasioned the arrest of Peter and John, it resulted in the conversion of an additional five thousand believers. The court heard still another discourse and forbade the disciples to preach or teach in the name of Jesus. All the centuries since have celebrated Peter's answer: "Whether it is right in the sight of God to listen to you rather than to God, you must judge, for we cannot but speak of what we have seen and heard" (4:19-20).

These words have ministered to thousands in history as men and women have committed themselves to the will of God. Recently, an unmarried missionary to a remote tribe in the Amazon asked my advice on her career. Her family was determined that she return to their home and care for their widowed mother. There were three other married children in the town with her mother, but they were fixed on the idea of this unmarried woman assuming the responsibility of their mother. I simply quoted to her Acts 4:19-20, and she felt it applied directly to her situation.

When Peter and John reported to the church the threat from the court, "they lifted their voices together to God" and requested that more signs and wonders accompany their work in order to spread the good news. Then "when they had prayed, the place in which they were gathered together was shaken, and they were all filled with the Holy Spirit and continued to speak the word of God with boldness" (4:31).

The greed of Ananias and Sapphira caused Peter to label their subterfuge a lie, not to men, but to God. He told Sapphira that they were actually testing the Spirit of the Lord. Both died on the spot (5:1-11).

When the problem over the distribution of food to the Hellenistic widows arose, the apostles had the congregation appoint seven men to oversee that work in order to relieve the apostles of the responsibility. After the choosing of the Seven, the apostles told the group, "But we will devote ourselves to prayer and to the ministry of the word" (6:4). They knew that their preaching depended on the great commandment of Jesus to pray. The leaders then prayed and laid their hands on the Seven (6:1-6). *Even the management of smaller logistical details depended on prayer.* We are immediately told that "the word of God continued to increase" (6:7). The apostles obeyed Jesus' commandments about prayer in the Last Discourse, and the church grew rapidly.

When Stephen was tried, his defense included a reference to God's hearing the groaning of the Israelites (7:34) and to their idolatrous sacrifice, certainly an insidious, false prayer (7:41). At Stephen's execution, the heavens were opened and he saw Jesus standing at the right hand of God. As the crowd stoned him, he cried two prayers: "Lord Jesus, receive my spirit" and then in imitation of his Lord, "Lord, do not hold this sin against them" (7:54-60). Both prayers indicate how much Stephen had absorbed the character of his Lord.

After the persecution of Stephen, God scattered the church over Judea and Samaria. Philip, one of the Seven, brought joy to a Samaritan city by miracles, and there he preached the Messiah. Hearing about this, the apostles in Jerusalem sent Peter and John to the city, who prayed for the converts to receive the Holy Spirit, for "they had only been baptized in the name of the Lord Jesus" (8:16).

A local sorcerer, Simon, offered the apostles money to procure this ability to bestow the Spirit. Peter reprimanded his doing so, saying, "Repent, therefore, of this wickedness of yours, and pray to the Lord that, if possible, the intent of your heart may be forgiven you" (8:22). Simon must have understood because in his fright he requested the apostles to pray for him (8:24). As the disciples returned to Jerusalem, they evangelized many Samaritan villages (8:25). We can be sure that prayer accompanied all these mighty works as the work of the church began.

Visions and appearances of the Lord characterized the entire apostolic period. After Saul's Damascus road experience, the Lord appeared to Ananias and told him to place his hands on Saul so that his blind eyes could see. While he was praying, Saul saw a vision of Ananias coming to help him. After Saul's miraculous healing, his subsequent witness necessitated an escape in a large basket by night from Damascus (9:10-25).

In Lydda, Peter healed a paralyzed man, telling him, "Aeneas, Jesus Christ heals you." This miracle brought mass conversions (9:32-35). Advised of the death of a beloved believer, Peter "knelt down, and prayed; and turning to the body he said, 'Tabitha [the Hebrew name], arise'" (9:40). As word of this resuscitation spread throughout Joppa, many came to faith in Christ.

The next vision, strangely, came not to an apostle but to a God-fearing Gentile, a Roman centurion named Cornelius, who "prayed continually to God." The angel told him to send to Joppa for Peter. The next day, Peter, in the midst of prayer (10:9), saw a vision that told him to open the kingdom door to Gentiles. Peter obeyed and preached the gospel to the Gentiles. To the amazement of the Jews, the Holy Spirit was poured out on their Gentile hearers (10:1-48). Later, when Jews in Jerusalem heard about this Gentile movement, they criticized Peter, who justified his vision by announcing that it came during prayer (11:5). When the Christian Jews heard this, "they glorified God, saying, 'Then to the Gentiles also God has granted repentance that leads to life'" (11:18).

After Herod killed the apostle James, he also imprisoned Peter, "but prayer was being made earnestly to God for him by the church" (12:5, HCSB). When the angel released Peter, he went immediately to the house of Mary, John Mark's mother, "where many were gathered together and were praying" (12:12). Peter told them to report his miraculous release to James, the Lord's brother, and Peter departed to another place.

Prayer initiated the missionary movement. Barnabas and Saul first received the call to go overseas, but they waited for the church in Antioch to move.

> While they were worshiping the Lord and fasting, the Holy Spirit said, "Set apart for me Barnabas and Saul for the work to which I *have called* them" [they already were aware of the call!]. Then after fasting and praying they laid their hands on them and sent them off. (13:2-3, emphasis added)

This call led to the proclamation of the word in Cyprus,[1] then in Antioch of Pisidia, Iconium, Lystra, Pamphylia, Perga, and Attalia. In Antioch, Gentile converts remained faithful when Judaizers stirred up a resistance there. Nevertheless, "the [converted] disciples were filled with joy and with the Holy Spirit" (13:52). The great missionary movement was now underway. In Lystra, God healed a lame man through Paul. This resulted in an abortive attempt to worship him; Paul stifled it (14:8-18). In every church the apostles appointed elders and prayed with them with fasting (13:4–14:23).

Saul, who from this time on was called Paul (13:9), selected Silas for this second missionary journey. In Philippi, they went to a place of prayer by the river and won Lydia to their cause. Later, on their way to prayer, they encountered a slave girl with a spirit of divination and cast the demon out of her. This caused her owner to bring about their arrest.

God miraculously opened the prison doors as Paul and Silas were praying and singing hymns at midnight (16:16-34), which in turn brought about the conversion of the Philippian jailor.

In Athens, Paul proclaimed the one true God, which resulted in a few conversions (17:22-34). He always used his various circumstances to proclaim Christ. The prayers of Acts were bearing fruit. When Paul met resistance in Corinth, the Lord encouraged him in a night vision (18:9-10).

Once again in Ephesus, "God was doing extraordinary miracles by the hands of Paul" (19:11). Paul escaped a riot caused by Demetrius, who made shrines for the goddess Artemis, and then Paul continued an extensive journey. In his last trip to Ephesus, he was aware that he was ending the missionary part of his ministry. At Miletus, he knelt down and prayed with the sorrowing church, which was grieved over his word that he would not see them again (20:36-38). This scene was repeated in Tyre, where Paul knelt down on the beach, prayed, and said good-bye to those of the church there.

In Cenchreae, Paul took a vow (so a vow is legitimate for New Testament Christians) and shaved his head. His total dependence on God showed when he assured the Ephesians that he would return to them "if God wills" (18:21). Later in Ephesus, Paul had to confront some Jewish exorcists who were falsely using Jesus' name; they received violent treatment from the demonized. "And fear fell upon them all, and the name of the Lord Jesus was extolled" (19:13-17).

Once Paul was again in Jerusalem, the believers glorified God over his missionary report (21:20). However, his presence in the temple caused a riot and a trial before the Sanhedrin. The following night, God granted Paul the encouraging word that he would eventually testify in Rome. Plot after plot to kill Paul failed; arrests and trials followed, but Paul knew that circumstances would not prevent his appearance before the emperor. In Caesarea before Festus, knowing his ultimate destiny, Paul appealed to Caesar (25:10-11). In his trial before Agrippa, who questioned Paul intently, Paul told the king, "Whether short or long, I would to God that not only you but also all who hear me this day might become such as I am — except for these chains" (26:29). Paul even prayed for his captors.

The decision was made to send Paul (and other prisoners) to Rome, via a ship. But during a storm the ship was set off course and Paul was granted another vision, which enabled him to assure the sailors. On the fourteenth day of the storm, Paul urged the men to take some food, "for not a hair is to perish from the head of any of you" (27:34). This amazing faith was to see him all the way to Caesar.

The storm caused even the sailors to pray for daylight (27:29). (Did they pray to the God of their captive?) The shipwreck landed them on Malta, where Publius, the father of the leading man of the island, was critically ill. Paul prayed, laid his hands on him, and God healed the old man. Many on the island who had diseases came to Paul and he generously healed them, obviously through prayer.

The last recorded prayer in Acts happened after Paul arrived safely in Rome. Some believers came to him "as far as the Forum of Appius and Three Taverns to meet us. On seeing them, Paul thanked God and took courage" (28:15). Luke tells us only that Paul stayed two years in his own house, "proclaiming the kingdom of God and teaching about the Lord Jesus Christ with all boldness and without hindrance" (28:31).

Chapter Fifteen

ROMANS, CORINTHIANS

KEY PRAYER VERSES FOR ROMANS

Paul gave us one of the most reassuring verses in the Bible in this key verse:

> For we do not know what to pray for as we ought, but the Spirit himself intercedes for us with groanings too deep for words. And he who searches hearts knows what is the mind of the Spirit, because the Spirit intercedes for the saints according to the will of God. (8:26-27)

Later, Paul, with his "thorn in the flesh," learned that God's strength was made perfect in his weakness (2 Corinthians 12:9) so that Paul would not even boast about special revelations (2 Corinthians 12:5). What a lesson for us in our self-centeredness!

KEY PRAYER THEME FOR ROMANS

The Intercession of the Lord Jesus and the Holy Spirit, with Many Thanksgivings (8:15,26-27,34)

Paul used a prayer in the greetings of his letters. He opened Romans with, "Grace to you and peace from God our Father and the Lord

Jesus Christ" (1:7). He then thanked God that the news of the believers' faith received worldwide report. He told them that he constantly mentioned them, always asking in his prayers that he might come to them (1:9-10). God answered this prayer in a way that Paul did not expect—an imprisonment—but the answer to his prayer was still a "yes."

The next specific mention of prayer comes after five chapters, which contain much of the material on grace and justification. In 6:17, Paul returned to his theme of thanksgiving: "But thanks be to God, that you who were once slaves of sin have become obedient from the heart to the standard of teaching to which you were committed." After his famous passage on sin (7:7-23), he concluded, "Wretched man that I am! Who will deliver me from this body of death? Thanks be to God through Jesus Christ our Lord!" (7:24-25).

In all of Paul's letters he dispensed grace and peace; he frequently expressed thanksgiving, all in the form of prayer. Perhaps his is the most radical conversion in history, and significantly, his teaching on prayer ranks second only to that of Jesus. Only Paul could write, from the depths of his own experience, that "the peace of God, which surpasses all understanding, will guard your hearts and your minds in Christ Jesus" (Philippians 4:7). What an integrated mind Paul had!

Chapter 8 nearly matches John 3:16 in the hearts of believers. Paul introduced the profundity of our adoption in 8:15-17:

> For you did not receive the spirit of slavery to fall back into fear, but you have received the Spirit of adoption as sons, by whom we cry, "Abba! Father!" The Spirit himself bears witness with our spirit that we are children of God, and if children, then heirs—heirs of God and fellow heirs with Christ.

The use of the family Aramaic word *Abba*, followed by the explanatory *pater* (Father) probably came from Jesus' teaching. In

Gethsemane, Jesus used *Abba* (Mark 14:36) and taught us in the Model Prayer to call God "Father." Paul carefully explained our joint heirship with Christ. Our sonship, however, is by adoption (8:23). Jesus' sonship is inherent in His having the same essence as the Father. We are finite; He is infinite. This family membership is emphasized again in 8:29, which tells us we were predestined to be conformed to the image of God's Son, "so that He would be the firstborn among many brothers" (HCSB).

Waiting, enjoined in Acts, assumes cosmic proportions in this great chapter: "For the creation waits with eager longing for the revealing of the sons of God" (8:19).

Waiting on the redemption of our bodies may be agonizing, and so we must use our "waiting" time for productive kingdom purposes.

Additional encouragement comes in 8:26-27:

> Likewise the Spirit helps us in our weakness. For we do not know what to pray for as we ought, but the Spirit himself intercedes for us with groanings too deep for words. And he who searches hearts knows what is the mind of the Spirit, because the Spirit intercedes for the saints according to the will of God.

Neither our weakness nor our mistakes count against us when we pray. God's own Spirit translates our prayer into those matters that count with God. In my own prayers, I ask that the Holy Spirit "retool" my prayer (I often feel awkward in my prayers) and conform my intention to the Father's pleasure.

As if the Spirit's intercession were not enough, Paul assured us in his next paragraph, "[Jesus] is at the right hand of God, who indeed is interceding for us" (8:34). That paragraph ends with the reassurance that nothing "will be able to separate us from the love of God in Christ Jesus our Lord" (8:39). God provided Romans 8 to be one of the most reassuring chapters in the Bible for Christians.

After giving this assurance, Paul abruptly shifted the focus to his sorrow for his fellow Israelites. He prayed that he would be cut off from the Messiah for the benefit of his countrymen (9:3). Paul knew the impossibility of such a wish but he used hyperbole to emphasize the depth of his concern. He reiterated this in 10:1: "Brothers, my heart's desire and prayer to God for them is that they might be saved." In the following chapter (11:3), he referred to Elijah's pleading for Israel (1 Kings 19:10,14).

Paul concluded that Israel's rejection had resulted in the Gentile reception of Christ, "that they also now may receive mercy" (11:31, HCSB). As Paul reflected on God's mercy to all, he penned one of the most glorious doxologies in the Bible:

Oh, the depth of the riches and wisdom and knowledge of God! How unsearchable are his judgments and how inscrutable his ways!

"For who has known the mind of the Lord,
    or who has been his counselor?"
"Or who has given a gift to him
    that he might be repaid?"

For from him and through him and to him are all things. To him be glory forever. Amen. (11:33-36)

Chapter 12 touches on prayer as we are asked "to present your bodies as a living sacrifice, holy and acceptable to God, which is your spiritual worship" (12:1). Paul was referring to our daily walk. Enoch and Noah walked with God. (Incidentally, that reminds us that appropriate bodily attitudes in prayer are standing, kneeling, or prostrating ourselves before God; all of them are walking with God.) It helps our "spiritual worship" to have our whole body participate in prayer times, as a symbol of our submission to God.

Chapter 14 urges us "not to quarrel over opinions" (14:1). In the process of naming uncertain issues, Paul advised,

> The one who observes the day, observes it [in prayer] in honor of the Lord. The one who eats, eats in honor of the Lord, since he gives thanks to God [in prayer], while the one who abstains, abstains in honor of the Lord and gives thanks to God [in prayer]. For none of us lives to himself, and none of us dies to himself. (14:6-7)

Paul celebrated God's mercy to all people with three praise hymns from the Gentiles in 15:9,11,12, quoting 2 Samuel 22:50, Psalm 18:49, Deuteronomy 32:43, and Isaiah 11:10. The apostle to the Gentiles never lost his loyalty to Israel, nor his concern for his own calling to the "pagans."

Paul's call for prayer from the Romans demonstrates his own conviction of the difficulty of prayer; it may be agonizing:

> I appeal to you, brothers, by our Lord Jesus Christ and by the love of the Spirit, to *strive together* with me in your prayers to God on my behalf, that I may be delivered from the unbelievers in Judea, and that my service for Jerusalem may be acceptable to the saints, so that by God's will I may come to you with joy and be refreshed in your company. (15:30-32, emphasis added)

Note that Paul asked that they "strive" in their prayers. Prayer may be work. He wrote the Colossians that Epaphras was "struggling on your behalf in his prayers" (Colossians 4:12). In my personal prayers, the intercessory part usually remains the hardest as I "strive" or "struggle" to be assured of the Holy Spirit's leading in a certain matter.

Paul ended Romans with another elaborate doxology praising the secret kept silent for long ages but then made known through the prophetic writings. He concluded, "To the only wise God be glory forevermore through Jesus Christ! Amen" (16:25-27).

KEY PRAYER VERSE FOR 1 CORINTHIANS

Paul stated a bedrock basis for all prayer, whether it be intercession, petition, praise, or any kind of communication with God, in 14:15 (our key verse):

> I will pray with my spirit, but I will pray with my mind also; I will sing praise with my spirit, but I will sing with my mind also.

This summary of the previous three chapters tells us that we are not to use a spiritless mind nor a mindless spirit. Prayer must make an intelligent use of all spiritual resources.

KEY PRAYER THEME FOR 1 CORINTHIANS

Prayer Should Involve Both the Spirit and the Mind
(chapters 12–14 and especially 14:13-17)
Paul's letter opens with a prayer for grace and peace (1:3) from God the Father and the Lord Jesus Christ, followed by a prayer of thanksgiving for the recipients of the letter because of God's grace operating in them (1:4-7).

Paul's Patience

The Corinthian letters and Galatians exhibit both Paul's patience and his steadfastness in prayer for those who opposed him. The churches were hounded by knotty problems and by attacks on Paul. He attacked every problem with aplomb and the certainty of his convictions.

Paul elaborated on the prayer theme of 1 Corinthians by quoting the key verse above (14:15; see 14:13-17). He wanted the entire being, mind, and spirit involved in prayer. To capture his thinking, study carefully all of chapters 12–14.

He did not return specifically to prayer until his discussion of marital relations when he commanded, "Do not deprive one another, except perhaps by agreement for a limited time, that you may devote yourselves to prayer" (7:5). Paul may have encountered, even in these early days of Christianity, Jesus' emphasis on the unity of His followers and agreement in prayer. Whatever background Paul had, he respected the spiritual aspect of marriage and encouraged it.

Still later, in treating the subject of eating food offered to idols, he invoked his spiritual freedom by specifying thanksgiving: "If I partake with thankfulness, why am I denounced because of that for which I give thanks?" (10:30). This tells us that regardless of what he ate or his manner of eating, Paul always pronounced a thanksgiving over his food: "So, whether you eat or drink, or whatever you do, do all to the glory of God" (10:31). Thanksgiving also uses the mind and the spirit.

KEY PRAYER VERSE FOR 2 CORINTHIANS

Paul set the tone for prayer early in this book as he appealed to the Corinthians for their prayers. After naming a few of the dangers he had escaped, he wrote,

> You also must help us by prayer, so that many will give thanks on our behalf for the blessing granted us through the prayers of many. (1:11)

Note once again the emphasis on thanksgiving that permeates Paul's writings.

KEY PRAYER THEME FOR 2 CORINTHIANS
Prayer Gives Help That Produces Thanksgiving (1:10-11; 4:15; 9:10-15)

The book begins with a prayer for grace and peace (1:2). Anticipating what he would be recounting of his own trials, Paul then launched into a doxology of the God of comfort: "Blessed be the God and Father of our Lord Jesus Christ, the Father of mercies and God of all comfort" (1:3). He explained that God's comfort in our trials helps us to comfort others.

Toward the end of the first chapter he introduced a strange adverb for Jesus, a word that most of us do not use for prayer: "For all the promises of God find their Yes [Greek, *Amen*] in him. That is why it is through him that we utter our Amen to God for his glory" (1:20). The original Hebrew for this word cannot be translated easily into other languages. *Amen* strongly affirms a statement or a prayer.

Jesus used it often to underline His words, "Truly [or 'verily,' but in the Greek, *amen*] I say to you . . ." In the book of John, Jesus often said "Amen, amen." The Old Testament often uses *amen* as an adjective modifying "God" (Isaiah 49:7; 65:16). Those writers brought the term to bear on the solidity of God's teachings, warnings, and promises (variously translated "trustworthy," "faithful," "truth," and others—Psalm 19:7; 111:7; Hosea 5:9).

When I was a youngster, my father used our daily family devotions to teach us that *amen* really meant "so be it." As I grew older and learned the power of the word in the original, I *began* my prayer at times, "Amen, Father, I pray . . ." and then ended with the same affirmation. I will even place this powerful word in the middle of my prayers. Understanding the full powerful gamut of meaning in the original will help our faith.

Paul briefly mentioned thanksgiving again, this time for God's putting him on display for spreading the knowledge of Christ (2:14). Paul never resented his many persecutions and various trials but again and again thanked the Lord in all circumstances. Small wonder that Christians in so many persecuted countries value so highly the word of God when they can extract encouraging examples like these! In 4:15-18 he explained this unusual phenomenon, once again in thanksgiving:

> For this light momentary affliction is preparing for us an eternal weight of glory [the Old Testament word for "glory," *kabod*, originally meant and continued to carry the meaning of "weight"] beyond all comparison, as we look not to the things that are seen but to the things that are unseen. For the things that are seen are transient, but the things that are unseen. (4:17-18)

Thanksgiving continues in 8:16, where Paul thanked God for Titus's diligence for the Corinthian believers. Paul elaborated on the generosity of the Corinthian church:

> For the ministry of this service is not only supplying the needs of the saints but is also overflowing in many thanksgivings to God. . . . They long for you and pray for you, because of the surpassing grace of God upon you. Thanks be to God for his inexpressible gift! (9:12,14-15)

Chapter 12 contains one of the Bible's "unanswered" prayers. Paul prayed with strong language: "I pleaded with the Lord three times [persistence again] to take it away from me" (12:8, HCSB). God also seemed not to answer immediately Job's plaints, and He denied David's plea for his baby's life. In the case of "unanswered" prayers, we may rest assured that God's wisdom is farseeing and accomplishes much that our shortened vision cannot immediately comprehend. God actually gave Paul a reason for His "no" answer: "My grace is sufficient for you, for my power is made perfect in weakness" (12:9). If Paul could have accomplished his astounding feats in his own strength, he might have taken credit for the conversions and healings he effected. God's work through his weakness filled Paul with thanksgiving.

I was born with a body temperature of 97.3, a low thyroid level, persistent anemia (the doctors tell me it is genetic and not correctable), many allergies, poor eyesight (I never saw a leaf on a tree until I got glasses at the age of five), a hiatal hernia, low blood pressure, and several other deficiencies that made me gawky and awkward. So it was easy, when God called me into His service, to understand that only God could do the work He was calling me to do, and that I must never rely on any natural abilities.

Only God can do His work; it is truly divine. In His strange love reaching to the lowest of us, He helps us participate with Him in His work (1 Corinthians 3:9). But we are junior partners and, like Paul, must depend on God's grace in His direction of our work. All of us would do well to realize that prayer is our most effective tool to do God's work.

Toward the end of his letter, Paul prayed for his coworkers in Corinth. Note the intensity of his prayer, a prayer every minister ought to memorize: "But we pray to God that you may not do wrong—not that we may appear to have met the test, but that you may do what is right, though we may seem to have failed" (13:7).

Paul concluded his letter with a Trinitarian prayer: "The grace of the Lord Jesus Christ and the love of God and the fellowship of the Holy Spirit be with you all" (13:14). It is interesting that the Trinitarian benediction gives three progressive blessings—the grace of Christ (the starting point for our grasp of His revelation), the love of God (the summary of all that He is), and finally, the fellowship of the Holy Spirit (that climax that provides even in this earthly life a foretaste of what is eternal).

The openings and closings of Paul's letters encapsulate rigorous doctrine in a moving exposure of his heart. In 1 Corinthians 13:13, he also used the number three—first faith, then hope, then love—again a progression. The entire Bible is an amazing progression: from "In the beginning, God," to "in the beginning was the Word," to the final prayer of the Bible, "Come, Lord Jesus."

Chapter Sixteen

GALATIANS THROUGH PHILEMON

KEY PRAYER VERSE FOR GALATIANS

In Romans, Paul emphasized intimacy with God by calling Him "Abba" (8:15). In Galatians, he did the same in our key verse:

> And because you are sons, God has sent the Spirit of his Son into our hearts, crying, *"Abba*, Father!"* (4:6, HCSB)

KEY PRAYER THEME FOR GALATIANS

The Role of the Holy Spirit in Communicating the Fatherhood of God (4:5-7)

Paul, as usual, introduced his letter with a prayer for grace and peace, and again credited God the Father and the Lord Jesus Christ as the bestower of these gifts. As he defended his apostleship, Paul affirmed that God, not the church officials in Judea, had given him his office. He declared, considering what he was about to write, "If I were still trying to please man, I would not be a servant of Christ" (1:10). But he added that the Judeans "glorified God because of me" (1:24), even though they knew his work only secondhand. Paul had an obsession for God's glory; glorifying is a major aspect of praise.

This firm yet gentle letter moves toward the climax of assuring the church of their heirship under God. Paul captured the children-of-God motif more fully than the writers of the Gospels, although both Matthew and Luke include Jesus' instructions to pray to the Father. In closing he offered a benedictory prayer for the grace of the Lord Jesus Christ to "be with" their spirit (6:18).

KEY PRAYER VERSES FOR EPHESIANS

The key verse for this book follows Paul's list of the armor of the Christian, and should be regarded as a culmination of his instruction on spiritual warfare. Paul had, in fact, started his list of the armor by naming the spiritual authorities that oppose us (6:12). We can imagine the intensity in the climactic command that the Ephesians heard after naming the armor. Paul told them they should always pray

> at all times in the Spirit, with all prayer and supplication. To that end keep alert with all perseverance, making supplication for all the saints, and also for me, that words may be given to me in opening my mouth boldly to proclaim the mystery of the gospel. (6:18-19)

We will see more on alertness in James 3.

KEY PRAYER THEME FOR EPHESIANS

Access to the Father Is Through Christ and the Holy Spirit
(1:15-21; 2:18; 3:12,14-21; 6:18-20)

This book's emphasis on prayer matches, in the Pauline letters, Luke's stress on prayer in the gospels. Prayer fills this letter, which Paul was writing from a prison in Rome. After his customary opening blessing, Paul added an additional blessing on God, "who has blessed us in Christ with every spiritual blessing in the heavenly places" (1:2-3). How astonishing to imagine that we can bless the Most Blessed! Even though we cannot fully comprehend it, Paul blessed God.[1] It had meaning for Paul, and so to God.

We sometimes limit our prayers to times of crises, but Paul filled his prayer for the Ephesian church with purely spiritual blessings:

> I do not cease to give thanks for you, remembering you in my prayers, that the God of our Lord Jesus Christ, the Father of glory, may give you the Spirit of wisdom and of revelation in the knowledge of him, having the eyes of your hearts enlightened, that you may know what is the hope to which he has called you, what are the riches of his glorious inheritance in the saints, and what is the immeasurable greatness of his power toward us who believe, according to the working of his great might. (1:16-19)

In his discussion of the unity of circumcised and uncircumcised, Paul explained the one legal right of entry that we all have through Christ and the Holy Spirit: "For through Him [Christ] we both have access by one Spirit to the Father" (2:18, HCSB). Our right of entry through Christ and the Holy Spirit is a major thrust of this letter. Later Paul reminds us that in Christ "we have boldness and access with confidence through our faith in him" (3:12).

Paul's concentration on the spiritual rather than the physical shows up once again in the same chapter:

> For this reason I bow my knees before the Father, from whom every family in heaven and on earth is named, that according to the riches of his glory he may grant you to be strengthened with power through his Spirit in your inner being, so that Christ may dwell in your hearts through faith — that you, being rooted and grounded in love, may have strength to comprehend with all the saints what is the breadth and length and height and depth, and to know the love of

Christ that surpasses knowledge, that you may be filled with all the fullness of God. (3:14-19)

To back up the enormous implications of this prayer, Paul immediately proceeded with a doxology to a God who will hear such profound emphasis on spirituality. This poem praises the power of prayer.

Now to him who is able to do far more abundantly than all that we ask or think, according to the power at work within us, to him be glory in the church and in Christ Jesus throughout all generations, forever and ever. Amen. (3:20-21)

After giving the command to be filled with the Spirit (5:18), Paul elaborated on the work of the Spirit in the congregation, telling us to use music and singing in our mutual conversation, and to give thanks for everything (5:19-20). After the key verse above, he reminded the congregation that he was an ambassador in chains and again asked prayer for boldness (6:19-20).

Paul's benediction at the end of his letter is more elaborate than most of the other closings. He prayed for peace, love with faith, and grace for all who "have undying love for our Lord Jesus" (6:23-24, HCSB).

KEY PRAYER VERSE FOR PHILIPPIANS

Although he was in chains, Paul advised the Philippian church,

Do not be anxious about anything, but in everything by prayer and supplication with thanksgiving let your requests be made known to God. (4:6)

Paul intended this as a reminder of his lifelong reliance on God rather than on his own abilities.

KEY PRAYER THEME FOR PHILIPPIANS
Joyful Confidence Should Characterize Our Prayers
(1:19; 3:1; 4:6,19)

The element of joy enters into Paul's salutation: "Always in every prayer of mine for you all making my prayer with joy" (1:4). In this greeting, he also prayed that the Philippians' "love will keep on growing in knowledge and every kind of discernment" (1:9, HCSB).

He even rejoiced in "rival" proclaimers who sought to trouble his imprisonment, because his rivals were proclaiming Christ: "What then? Only that in every way, whether in pretense or in truth, Christ is proclaimed, and in that I rejoice" (1:18).

Paul's personal life remained consistent with his admonitions to rejoice.

About the middle of his letter, Paul described joy as a "protection" for believers: "Finally, my brothers, rejoice in the Lord. To write the same things to you is no trouble to me and is safe for you" (3:1). He did not mind repeating himself. In 4:4 he reiterated, "Rejoice in the Lord always; again I will say, rejoice." This leads into the key verse above.

The church in Philippi evidently had sent a gift by Epaphroditus that Paul viewed as an offering to God Himself. He called it "a fragrant offering, a sacrifice acceptable and pleasing to God" (4:18).

Once again he closed his letter by praying the grace of the Lord Jesus Christ on the spirit of the Philippians (4:23). Certainly Christ's grace overwhelmed the body of believers there.

KEY PRAYER VERSE FOR COLOSSIANS

Practicing Christians can apply Paul's key verse:

> Continue steadfastly in prayer, being watchful in it with thanksgiving. (4:2)

Jesus had warned His disciples to stay awake in Gethsemane (Matthew 26:41). The psalmist waited for the Lord "more than watchmen for the morning" (Psalm 130:6). In His teaching, Jesus repeatedly emphasized attentive vigilance (Matthew 24:42; 26:41; Luke 12:47). Paul also gave priority to alertness (Ephesians 6:18; 2 Timothy 4:5).

Key Prayer Theme for Colossians
Our Greatest Intercession Should Be for Spiritual Purposes (1:3,9-12; 2:1-2)

Paul started his letter by informing the Colossian church that he was thanking God for them and praying for them (1:3). The following paragraph maintains his vigilance in prayer; in 1:9-12 Paul went into great detail about their growth and work in and for Christ:

> And so, from the day we heard, we have not ceased to pray for you, asking that you may be filled with the knowledge of his will in all spiritual wisdom and understanding, so as to walk in a manner worthy of the Lord, fully pleasing to him, bearing fruit in every good work and increasing in the knowledge of God. May you be strengthened with all power, according to his glorious might, for all endurance and patience with joy, giving thanks to the Father, who has qualified you to share in the inheritance of the saints in light.

In chapter 2 Paul emphasized his "great struggle" on their behalf, just as he had agonized for the Romans. He wanted them to have "all the riches of full assurance of understanding and the knowledge of God's mystery, which is Christ" (2:1-2). The spiritual nature of all Paul's prayers is striking. Paul's spirit dominated his physical being.

KEY PRAYER VERSE FOR 1 THESSALONIANS

The New Testament writers enjoin us several times to pray continually. The key prayer verse for 1 Thessalonians concerns continual prayer.

Pray without ceasing, give thanks in all circumstances; for this is the will of God in Christ Jesus for you. (5:17-18)

KEY PRAYER THEME FOR 1 THESSALONIANS
The Importance of Praying Continually
Paul jumped right into his main prayer theme:

We give thanks to God always for all of you, constantly mentioning you in our prayers, remembering before our God and Father your work of faith and labor of love and steadfastness of hope in our Lord Jesus Christ. (1:2-3)

This theme recurs throughout the book.

In the second chapter, he returned to this idea:

And we also thank God constantly for this, that when you received the word of God, which you heard from us, you accepted it not as the word of men but as what it really is, the word of God. (2:13)

The next chapter continues the idea of constantly thanking God for the Thessalonian church (3:9). Constancy is emphasized in Paul's claim that he prayed "earnestly *night and day* to see you face to face and to complete what is lacking in your faith" (3:10, HCSB, emphasis added). This emphasis on perseverance is consonant with Jesus' command to abide. If we abide, we persevere. Paul concluded with a prayer for the believers there and ended with "Amen" (3:11-13, HCSB).

Chapter 5 contains the key verse for this book. Paul concluded with another prayer for the believers in Thessalonica (5:23-25,28).

KEY PRAYER VERSE FOR 2 THESSALONIANS

The key prayer verse for this second letter to the Thessalonians continues the emphasis on constancy in prayer.

> To this end we always pray for you, that our God may make you worthy of his calling and may fulfill every resolve for good and every work of faith by his power. (1:11)

Intercession becomes the theme of the entire book.

KEY PRAYER THEME FOR 2 THESSALONIANS
Intercession for the Church

Paul continued his custom of thanking God again for the Thessalonians (1:2-3). He thanked God again in 2:13; surely the church understood his deep affection for them.

His first intercession comes in the same chapter. After naming God's blessings on the church, he prayed that God would comfort and establish them (2:16-17). We can pray these same intercessions today. The needs of Christians remain remarkably similar from century to century.

Paul began chapter 3 with a plea that the believers in Thessalonica pray for him — for his message and for deliverance from evil men. He believed in intercession not only for others but for himself.

The remainder of chapter 3 is largely intercession for the church. The three intercessions below are model biblical ways for us to intercede for our churches. Each could be applied to a local church.

May the Lord direct your hearts to the love of God and to the stead-fastness of Christ. (3:5)

Now may the Lord of peace himself give you peace at all times in every way. (3:16)

The grace of our Lord Jesus Christ be with you all. (3:18)

Paul's Personal Letters

Most of Paul's letters send greetings to people in the churches. Four of his letters are to individuals—three to pastors and one to a friend. Paul felt deeply involved with all those to whom he wrote. Each demonstrates profound love and concern for all his converts.

KEY PRAYER VERSE FOR 1 TIMOTHY

As stated in the introduction, the key prayer verse may vary from the prayer theme of a book. With the prayer verses, I looked to find key prayer ideas that would help Christians in their private and public prayer lives. Paul made an important imperative:

Therefore, I want the men in every place to pray, lifting up holy hands without anger or argument. (2:8, HCSB)

Paul wanted prayer to be universal in time and space.

KEY PRAYER THEME FOR 1 TIMOTHY
Everyone Should Pray

As usual, Paul introduced thanksgiving early in his letter (1:12) as well as a powerful doxology (1:17). Soon he enjoined,

> First of all, then, I urge that supplications, prayers, intercessions, and thanksgivings be made for all people, for kings and all who are in high positions, that we may lead a peaceful and quiet life, godly and dignified in every way. (2:1-2)

Note that Paul does not limit intercession to good rulers, but to "all those who are in high positions." I have often prayed for leaders and politicians I disagreed with. Prayer is efficacious with all authority. God can influence everyone under His sway (Proverbs 21:1).

The theme of constancy in prayer even shows in Paul's advice to church members. The widow puts all her hope in God and continues night and day in her petitions and prayers (5:5). Paul ended 1 Timothy with a benediction of grace.

KEY PRAYER VERSE FOR 2 TIMOTHY

Paul's spiritual affection for his children in the faith shows in his introduction:

> I thank God whom I serve, as did my ancestors, with a clear conscience, as I remember you constantly in my prayers night and day. (1:3)

KEY PRAYER THEME FOR 2 TIMOTHY
Spiritual Benedictions Can Be Administered Through Prayer

As he approached his death, Paul continued his prayers night and day, as he had advised his churches to do. He prayed not only for Timothy, but for his helper, Onesiphorus. Twice in 1:16-18, Paul prayed that the Lord would grant Onesiphorus mercy for his help. Paul concluded with a benediction, accompanied by grace, that the Lord be with Timothy.

KEY PRAYER VERSE FOR TITUS
Paul wrote as a parent to Titus:

> To Titus, my true child in a common faith:
> Grace and peace from God the Father and Christ Jesus our Savior (1:4).

KEY PRAYER THEME FOR TITUS
A Spiritual Parent Assumes Prayer Responsibility for the Life of a Spiritual Child
The parental aspect of Paul's relationship to Titus appears in the key verse above. The pastoral advice Paul gave him is evident throughout the letter. Paul concluded, as he normally did, with a prayer: "Grace be with you all" (3:15). The father-son relationship evidences itself in Paul's beginning and ending with a prayer for grace.

KEY PRAYER VERSES FOR PHILEMON
Paul mentioned faith in his introduction:

> I thank my God always when I remember you in my prayers, because I hear of your love and of the faith that you have toward the Lord Jesus and for all the saints. (verses 4-5)

Paul's concern for individuals equaled his concern in the pastoral letters.

KEY PRAYER THEME FOR PHILEMON
The Faith of Philemon Prompted Paul's Prayers

In verse 6, Paul repeated the faith theme. He prayed that Philemon's participation in the faith might become effective through knowing every good thing that is in us for the sake of Christ. In my own case, simply knowing many prayer champions has increased my faith. Are you inspiring others? Paul concluded with his usual prayer for grace: "The grace of the Lord Jesus Christ be with your spirit" (verse 25).

Every letter of Paul includes in his opening salutation the word "grace." Today many of our songs and choruses are about grace (for example, "Amazing Grace," popular in nearly all denominations). When it is not in the title of the hymn or chorus, "grace" occurs in the refrain ("Mercy there was great and grace was free" in "At Calvary"). Scripture itself abounds in statements or revelations of grace (1 Corinthians 15:10; 2 Corinthians 1:12). Paul spoke of the "immeasurable riches of his grace" (Ephesians 2:7). The often-used Aaronic blessing includes the central line, "The LORD make his face to shine upon you and be gracious to you" (Numbers 6:25).

Our hymns, choruses, and Scripture remind us so frequently of the grace of God that each of us needs to follow Paul's example in our appropriation of those "immeasurable riches" for the sake of a needy and hungering world watching us.

Chapter Seventeen

HEBREWS THROUGH JUDE

KEY PRAYER VERSES FOR HEBREWS

The key prayer verse for Hebrews should increase our faith as we pray.

> For we do not have a high priest who is unable to sympathize with our weaknesses, but one who in every respect has been tempted as we are, yet without sin. Let us then with confidence draw near to the throne of grace, that we may receive mercy and find grace to help in time of need. (4:15-16)

KEY PRAYER THEMES FOR HEBREWS

Hebrews, like Luke, has two predominating prayer themes. The writer's initial theme demonstrates God's sympathy for us.

Christ Makes Intercession for Us[1]

Early on, the writer introduced the theme of Christ's longsuffering with our sinful nature (2:18; 4:15-16). The consequence of Christ's care shows itself strongly in chapter 7: "Consequently, he is able to save to the uttermost those who draw near to God through him, since he always lives to make intercession for them" (7:25). Hebrews 9:24 emphasizes that Jesus intercedes for us in heaven itself. Christ inaugurated this access through "the holy places" (His flesh). He also functions as the Great High Priest for us, so we have confidence in His intercession, as the writer emphasized throughout the first ten chapters of Hebrews.

Hebrews and the Old Testament

The writer addressed the letter to the Jews, and the reader would profit from a study in any good Bible dictionary of the sacrifices and offerings of the Pentateuch and of the duties of the high priest. Christ fulfilled all that was foreshadowed in the first five books of the Bible.

Our confidence grows greater when we realize that, according to Romans 8:26, the Holy Spirit also is interceding for us. Furthermore, John emphasized Jesus' intercession for our sins in 1 John 2:1. So we have two great intercessors constantly pleading on our behalf—the Holy Spirit and the Lord Jesus Christ.

The Kind of Faith God Wants Us to Have

All this building of confidence through the first ten chapters leads to the summary definition of faith in 11:1: "Now faith is the assurance of things hoped for, the conviction of things not seen."

In chapter 3 of *Seeing the Unseen,* I give twenty-one translations of that difficult word *hypostasis,* here translated "assurance." The basic idea or totality of the meanings is "assurance," a synonym for "confidence." As is well known, Hebrews 11 lists men and women of faith. For us, what matters is that all these heroes of faith were real flesh-and-blood persons, with our weaknesses and strengths. God described this assurance or confidence in order for us to have that kind of faith.

In fact, verse 6 of this important chapter cautions us that it is impossible to please God without faith. Faith does not merely believe that God will answer, but rather it is complete confidence that God is who He says He is and that He is on our side. Many of my "unanswered" prayers led to results far better than my immediate request. God often "takes my side" in unexpected ways.

We must not take "ask, and it will be given to you" (Matthew 7:7; Luke 11:9) as a license to manipulate God but rather as an indication that God wants us to come to Him for our needs. Our basic needs are for spiritual growth. Matthew 7:7 occurs in the kingdom manifesto; most of the Sermon on the Mount concerns the kingdom and kingdom living, including this comprehensive but often misapplied statement.

God has given many literal answers to my specific requests, but in retrospect, I can see that *all* of God's answers have left me on a higher plane. Often the answer was in an unexpected area, one I would not have imagined, but far higher and better than I knew how to ask. God wants us to ask; asking indicates our dependence on Him for all of life.

My wife fought cancer for twenty-six years. Throughout the ordeal we prayed constantly for healing, and God often healed her. When the time came for God to take her to Himself, I had much to thank Him for, twenty-six years of it. And our family realized that God had spared her in this life in order for us to become more intimate with Him.

KEY PRAYER VERSE FOR JAMES

The key prayer verse for James contains two key ideas: "righteous" and "as it is working."

Confess your sins to one another and pray for one another, that you may be healed. The prayer of a righteous person has great power as it is working. (5:16)

"As it is working" can be translated "intense," "fervent," or "effectual." It conveys an idea of strength or might; it is related to our word *energy*. It implies sincerity. Obviously, God will give no attention to the prayer of the wicked, unless it is a prayer that will lead the pray-er to God. In other words, God does not heed a prayer that is not "real."

In *Seeing the Unseen,* I mention that I pray for a "sense of reality" to touch my prayers. When God intensifies my sense of reality, I am conscious of the following factors:[2]

- I sense the presence of the Holy Spirit mediating to the Father all I pray (Ephesians 5:18).
- I pray with the mind of Christ (1 Corinthians 2:16).
- I have a strong sense of onward progression. The Spirit is leading me what to pray for (Philippians 3:13-14).
- I am filled with a deep, strong desire to please the Father. I cannot ask for something foreign to the holiness of God (John 8:29).
- I have a strong sense that nothing is impossible with omnipotence (Matthew 21:21). Elijah even had the people pour gallons of water on the sacrifice before the fire fell (1 Kings 18:33).
- My thoughts are entirely concentrated on God. He hears (Ephesians 4:5-6).
- I seriously *want* the effects God wants to bring about and I feel a strong confidence that my desires are springing from the desires of the Father (Matthew 6:10).

KEY PRAYER THEME FOR JAMES

We Should Pray for All the Basic Needs of Life[3]

James started by advising us to pray for wisdom. He elaborated on the importance of faith in making this prayer (1:5-8). Although several Bible books address faith (Romans, Hebrews), James took a different tack, discussing for four verses the instability of one who does not pray in faith.

In 4:2-3, he gave another weakness in our prayers—praying with selfish motives: "You ask and do not receive, because you ask wrongly, to spend it on your passions" (4:3). The setting of Matthew 7:7 has already hinted that effective prayer depends on knowing the character of God and seeking the kingdom.

Toward the end of the book, James summarized his injunction that we should pray about everything.

> Is anyone among you suffering? Let him pray. Is anyone cheerful? Let him sing praise. Is anyone among you sick? Let him call for the elders of the church, and let them pray over him, anointing him with oil in the name of the Lord. And the prayer of faith will save the one who is sick, and the Lord will raise him up. And if he has committed sins, he will be forgiven. Therefore, confess your sins to one another and pray for one another, that you may be healed. (5:13-16)

He argued his case by telling us that Elijah had no advantage over us except fervency. The Bible intends to inspire ordinary people by using other ordinary people as examples. Some Christians feel inadequate in their prayers. God wants us to pray—so much that He encourages us to use the family name "Abba" in Romans 8:15 and Galatians 4:6. We could hardly be more common than Peter and Amos.

KEY PRAYER VERSE FOR 1 PETER

Peter stressed seriousness of purpose in prayer; the key prayer verse makes this obvious:

> The end of all things is at hand; therefore be self-controlled and sober-minded for the sake of your prayers. (4:7)

KEY PRAYER THEME FOR 1 PETER

Prayer Requires Seriousness of Purpose

Here is a list of Peter's injunctions on prayer:

- Address God as Father in fear (not merely being afraid, but in profound reverence; 1:17).
- Husbands, honor your wives so that your prayers will not be hindered (3:7).
- The eyes and ears of the Lord attend to the prayer of the righteous (3:12).
- Be self-controlled and of sober spirit for the purpose of prayer (4:7).
- If you are persecuted, glorify God (4:16).
- Cast all your anxiety on the Lord (5:7).
- To God be dominion forever (5:11).
- Peace be to all who are in Christ (5:14).

Every one of these injunctions was of vital importance in the first century and continues to be so today.

KEY PRAYER VERSE FOR 2 PETER

If we fail to appreciate the magnitude of God's promises, Peter reminded us,

By [his glory and excellence] he has granted to us his precious and very great promises, so that through them you may become partakers of the divine nature. (1:4)

KEY PRAYER THEME FOR 2 PETER
God's Promises Are Magnificent

The key verse above shows the prayer theme for this little book. Through these promises, we actually become partakers of the divine nature. We are joint heirs with Christ. We cannot spend an eternity with perfect holiness unless we are partaking of God's nature.

In common with Paul, Peter began and ended the letter with a prayer. The salutation blesses his readers and the conclusion states a beautiful doxology on Christ—a fitting framework to contain the reference to God's magnificent promises.

KEY PRAYER VERSE FOR 1 JOHN

First John delays the main prayer verse until near the end of the book.

And this is the confidence that we have toward him, that if we ask anything according to his will he hears us. And if we know that he hears us in whatever we ask, we know that we have the requests that we have asked of him. (5:14-15)

If you practice the seven suggestions mentioned in the material on James, you discover with the passage of time that usually you are praying "according to His will." God knows when to reveal His will to you, and you will be surprised at the confidence—or faith—that enters into your prayer:

Beloved, if our heart does not condemn us, we have confidence before God; and whatever we ask we receive from him, because we keep his commandments and do what pleases him. (3:21-22)

KEY PRAYER THEME FOR 1 JOHN
We Should Pray with Confidence

According to our key verse, confidence comes naturally when we are fellowshipping with God. This involves spending time with Him. The book of Romans assures us that the Holy Spirit intercedes for us (Romans 8:26) and Hebrews tells us that Jesus also prays for us (Hebrews 7:25). How stunning that both the Spirit and the Lord Jesus are interceding for us! That should inspire confidence.

In addition, we have the assurance that Jesus prays for us specifically in our sins (2:1). John tells us to confess our sins, and God is faithful and just to forgive them. In fact, He will not remember our sins (Hebrews 10:17). When sin occurs, the Lord Jesus acts as our advocate with the Father (2:1). We fellowship with Him by keeping His commandments and by doing what is pleasing in His sight.

KEY PRAYER VERSE AND THEME FOR 2 JOHN
A Greeting Can Be a Prayer

The only prayer in this brief letter is in the salutation:

> Grace, mercy, and peace will be with us, from God the Father and from Jesus Christ the Father's Son, in truth and love. (verse 3)

Try to fathom how first- and second-century saints plumbed the depths of God revealed by the last living apostle!

KEY PRAYER VERSE AND THEME FOR 3 JOHN
The Right Spiritual Stance Also Enables Prayer for Well-Being

Both 2 and 3 John have a prayer in the greeting. John prayed in his third letter,

> Beloved, I pray that all may go well with you and that you may be in good health, as it goes well with your soul. (verse 2)

John was concerned with the whole person, not just the spirit. He prayed for the prosperity and health of his friend.

KEY PRAYER VERSE FOR JUDE

Jude emphasized the role of the Holy Spirit:

> But you, beloved, building yourselves up in your most holy faith and praying in the Holy Spirit. (verse 20)

We cannot pray in the Spirit if we are not filled with the Spirit.

KEY PRAYER THEME FOR JUDE
All Glory Should Be to God Through the Lord Jesus Christ

The conclusion of Jude praises the Father and the Son in another magnificent doxology:

> Now to him who is able to keep you from stumbling and to present you blameless before the presence of his glory with great joy, to the only God, our Savior, through Jesus Christ our Lord, be glory, majesty, dominion, and authority, before all time and now and forever. Amen. (verses 24-25)

Jude used an unusual opening to his doxology: "able to keep you from stumbling." Most of the letters begin with a personal salutation or greeting to the church or area being addressed. Even the Model Prayer begins with "our Father." Jude was creative. This letter bears no rituality.

The resounding doxology at the end would well fit any Christian's desire to praise God. It could function as the climax for a book or discussion of prayer. Prayer serves not to fit our dreams or purposes, but God's. Because God initiated prayer, all prayer is made through, to, and for God.

Chapter Eighteen

REVELATION

KEY PRAYER VERSE FOR REVELATION

Throughout the book of Revelation, many and various groups offered praise to the Lord. The key prayer verse summarizes all these series.

> And I heard every creature in heaven and on earth and under the earth and in the sea, and all that is in them, saying, "To him who sits on the throne and to the Lamb be blessing and honor and glory and might forever and ever!" (5:13)

KEY PRAYER THEME FOR REVELATION

All Creation Will Worship and Praise the Lord

No other Bible book approaches the consummate worship and praise that Revelation does. The word *worship* (of the Lord) occurs seven times, the past tense *worshipped* three times, and the word *glory* (of the Lord) appears seventeen times. The opening chapter has the membership in the kingdom proclaiming "to him be glory and dominion forever and ever. Amen" (1:6). This book puts our finiteness in perspective to God's infinity.

Joy Accompanies Praise

In the Old Testament, the word *joy* appears 119 times and *rejoice* 71 times. In the New Testament, *joy* occurs 60 times and *rejoice* 7 times. It was the major prayer theme in Deuteronomy and an important theme in Philippians. Joy accompanies praise. Happiness is a continuing state, and joy is a punctuation mark. *Glory* appears 202 times in the Old Testament and 161 times in the New Testament, indicating its importance. *Glad* occurs 71 times in the Old Testament and *merry* 9 times in the New Testament.

The four living creatures set in motion an enchanting series of phrases of praise and worship. Significantly, they began with the triple holiness of the seraphim in Isaiah 6:3:

> Holy, holy, holy, is the Lord God Almighty,
>> who was and is and is to come! (Revelation 4:8)

The creatures incorporated into the Trisagion (thrice holy) the eternality of God, which Jesus had declared in 1:8.

In response, the twenty-four elders, with bowls of incense that are the prayers of the saints, sang,

> Worthy are you, our Lord and God,
>> to receive glory and honor and power,
> for you created all things,
>> and by your will they existed and were created. (4:11)

The bowls of incense indicate that these prayers became tangible when they left the lips of the pray-ers. They are incense to God, who loves the pleasing aroma of the sacrifices made to Him.[1] The indescribable sacrifice of Christ was "a fragrant offering and sacrifice to God" (Ephesians 5:2). Even today "we are the aroma of Christ to God among those who are being saved" (2 Corinthians 2:15). Our prayers are incense to God! Their song praises the worth of Christ. This praise of Christ's worth recurs four more times throughout Revelation (4:11; 5:2,4,12).

Several references refer to Christ's worthiness to open the scroll with seven seals. The second reference has one of the twenty-four elders proclaiming,

> Worthy are you to take the scroll
>   and to open its seals,
> for you were slain, and by your blood you ransomed people for God
>   from every tribe and language and people and nation. (5:9)

The praise was taken up by many angels, "myriads of myriads and thousands of thousands" who amplify the worth with multiple attributions of praise:

> "Worthy is the Lamb who was slain, to receive power and wealth and wisdom and might and honor and glory and blessing!" And I heard *every* creature in heaven and on earth and under the earth and in the sea, and all that is in them, saying, "To him who sits on the throne and to the Lamb be blessing and honor and glory and might forever and ever!" And the four living creatures said, "Amen!" and the elders fell down and worshiped. (5:12-14, emphasis added)

Chapter 6 introduces the first prayer as an actual plea. The souls of believers who had been slain for their faith cried with a loud voice, "O Sovereign Lord, holy and true, how long before you will judge and avenge our blood on those who dwell on the earth?" (6:10). The Lord told them to wait a little longer.

The praise continues in chapter 7. This time a multitude from the Tribulation cried, "Salvation belongs to our God who sits on the throne, and to the Lamb!" (7:10). At this sudden occurrence, the angels, elders, and living creatures fell on their faces and worshipped God, saying, "Amen! Blessing and glory and wisdom and thanksgiving [thanksgiving was a part of the praise] and honor and power and might be to our God forever and ever! Amen" (7:12). Note that they began with "Amen."

Immediately after the seven angels received seven trumpets, another angel was holding a golden censer. He took much incense and added it to the prayers to God. John added, "Then the angel took the censer and filled it with fire from the altar and threw it on the earth, and there were peals of thunder, rumblings, flashes of lightning, and an earthquake" (8:5). This prayer saw an immediate answer.

In chapter 11, John wrote that a terrifying earthquake followed the ascension of the two witnesses. Terrified, the survivors "gave glory to the God of heaven" (verse 13). After the seventh angel sounded his trumpet, a loud voice in heaven announced that the kingdom of the world had come under the dominion of God. His eternal reign was now a visible fact. At that, the twenty-four elders again prostrated themselves and began their paean of praise with thanksgiving:

> We give thanks to you, Lord God Almighty,
>   who is and who was,
> for you have taken your great power
>   and begun to reign. (11:17)

Before Satan's overthrow, a loud voice in heaven proclaimed, "Therefore, rejoice, O heavens and you who dwell in them!" (12:12). Chapter 14 saw a very special song before the throne, the four living creatures, and the twenty-four elders, but no one could learn the song except the 144,000 who had been purchased from the earth (14:3).

Four verses later, John wrote that another angel proclaimed the eternal gospel to all the inhabitants of the earth, saying, "Fear God and give him glory, because the hour of his judgment has come, and worship him who made heaven and earth, the sea and the springs of water (14:7). This part of the drama came to a climax with a voice from heaven proclaiming, "Blessed are the dead who die in the Lord from now on" (14:13).

In chapter 15, the seven angels began the last of the plagues. John wrote that he saw a sea of glass mixed with fire; beside the sea were those who had come off victorious over the beast and the number of its name. And they sang,

> Great and amazing are your deeds,
>> O Lord God the Almighty!
> Just and true are your ways,
>> O King of the nations!
> Who will not fear, O Lord,
>> and glorify your name?
> For you alone are holy.
>> All nations will come
>> and worship you,
> for your righteous acts have been revealed. (15:3-4)

When the third angel poured his bowl into the waters, they became putrid with blood. The angel of the waters proclaimed (note that an angel can pray),

> Just are you, O Holy One, who is and who was,
>> for you brought these judgments.
> For they have shed the blood of saints and prophets,
>> and you have given them blood to drink.
> It is what they deserve! (16:5-6)

John writes that he heard the altar saying,

Yes, Lord God the Almighty,
    true and just are your judgments! (16:7)

As the book comes to a climax, a great multitude in heaven alternated with voices from the creatures and elders:

"Hallelujah!
Salvation and glory and power belong to our God,
    for his judgments are true and just;
for he has judged the great prostitute
    who corrupted the earth with her immorality,
and has avenged on her the blood of his servants."

Once more they cried out,

"Hallelujah!
The smoke from her goes up forever and ever." (19:1-3)

The creatures and the elders prostrated themselves with a hearty "Amen. Hallelujah!" (19:4).

John was almost at a loss for words as he described a great multitude as the sound of many waters answering,

Hallelujah!
For the Lord our God
    the Almighty reigns.
Let us rejoice and exult
    and give him the glory,
for the marriage of the Lamb has come,
    and his Bride has made herself ready;

it was granted her to clothe herself
    with fine linen, bright and pure. (19:6-8)

An important aside happened when John wrote that he fell at the feet of an angel. The angel rejoined that he was merely a servant of the prophets and those heeding the words of this book. He cautioned John, "Worship God" (19:10).

We can imagine the burning in John's heart as he responded to Jesus' words that He was coming quickly,

Amen. Come, Lord Jesus!
    The grace of the Lord Jesus be with all. Amen. (22:20-21)

At present, all of God's world echoes this prayer, so poignant in persecuted countries. May all God's people cry out John's final prayer, the last prayer in the Bible.

Since so many of Paul's salutations prayed for grace, we may, too. Grace has always marked God's dealings with His people. He gives it freely as a part of His nature. God chose to end the Bible with it. May every reader call out to God Almighty the ending of His own word:

Come, Lord Jesus!
    The grace of the Lord Jesus be with all. Amen. (22:20-21)

ALL THE PRAYERS OF THE BIBLE

This appendix lists all the ways God and humankind communicated, including altars, sacrifices, confession, the cries of humanity, the various dialogues between God and people, requests, thanksgiving, worship, praise, and the sharing of joy.

OLD TESTAMENT

Genesis	16:13	27:28-29
3:9-14,17-19	17:1-2,17-21	28:3-4
4:3	18:2-3,13-14	28:16-22
4:26	18:23-32	29:35
6:9	19:27-28	30:17
8:20-21	20:6-7,17	30:22
9:24-27	21:12-13	31:24
12:7-9	21:33	32:9-12
13:3-4	24:12-15	32:24-30
13:18	24:26-27	33:20
14:18-20	24:59-60	35:3-7
15:2-6	25:21-23	40:8
15:7-8,18	26:24-25	43:14

46:2-4

Exodus
2:23-24
3:1-14
4:1-17
4:31
5:21,22-23
8:12-13
8:30-31
9:33
10:18-19
14:10
15:1-18
15:21
15:24-25
17:4-6
18:10-11
19:3
19:17
19:19
19:23
22:22-23
23:14-25
25:17-22
28:30
30:1-7
30:34-36
32:11-14
32:31-32
33:11
33:12-23
34:5-9

34:28
34:34-35
40:26-27

Leviticus
1:3-9
1:17
2:1-2,9
4:1-35
5:14-19
8:1-36
9:22
17:6
23:40

Numbers
6:22-27
7:89
8:21
10:35-36
11:2
11:17
11:21-23,31,33
12:11-16
14:13-25
16:15
16:22-24
16:41-50
17:7
20:16
21:2
21:7
21:16-18

22:10-12,20-35
23:3-5,16
24:1-25
27:5-7
27:15-21
31:48-54

Deuteronomy
3:23-28
4:7
8:2
8:10
9:18-20,25-29
10:10-11
10:21
12:5-7
12:12
12:18
14:23
14:26
15:9
16:10-11
16:16
26:3-11
27:7
27:12-26
32:1-4
32:48-52
33:1-29
34:10

Joshua
2:11-14,20

5:6

5:13-15

7:6-15

7:24-26

8:30-31,33

9:14,18-19

10:12-14

18:6

18:8,10

19:51

21:45

22:10,16,19,6-28,34

24:1

Judges

1:1-2

2:4-5

3:9,15

4:3

5:1-31

6:6-8,10

6:11-24

6:36-40

7:15

10:10-16

11:10-11

11:27

11:30-31,39

13:8-25

15:8-19

16:28

20:1,9,18,23

20:26-28

21:1-4

Ruth

1:8-9,17

2:4

2:12

2:19-20

3:10

4:11,14-15

1 Samuel

1:10-17,19-20

1:22-23

1:26-28

2:1-11

2:20-21

3:1-10

4:3-11

6:15

7:2-11

7:17

8:6-7

8:18-19,21

9:9

9:15-16

9:17-19,22-24,27

10:8a

11:15

12:3,5-7,10,16-19,

22-23

13:9, 13

14:8-10

14:35,37,41,44-45

15:10-11

15:24-31

15:33

16:2

21:7

22:9-10

23:1-4,5c

23:10-13

23:16-18

23:21

24:12,15,19-22a

25:22,32-33,39

28:6

30:6-8

2 Samuel

1:12

2:1,5-6

3:9-10

3:29

3:35,39

5:3

5:19-20

5:23-25

6:5-7,11

6:14-18,20-23

7:18-29

8:11

10:12

12:13

12:16,20

13:25

14:11,17

15:7-8,12
15:21
19:7
19:13
21:1,3,5-7,9
21:14
22:1-51
23:16-17
24:10,17-25

1 Kings
1:5-9
1:17,29,36-37
1:47-48
2:23-24
2:42-43
3:5-15
5:7
8:12-15
8:16-21
8:22-65
9:3
9:25
10:9
13:6
17:12-16
17:20-24
18:26
18:36-39
18:41-46
19:4
19:8-18
22:3-8,15-18

2 Kings
1:10,12
2:4
2:14
2:19-24
3:11,15-18
4:1-7
4:15-17
4:27,32-37
4:38-44
5:8-14
5:15-17
5:20-27
6:5-7
6:17-18
8:8-15
13:4
19:4
19:14-35
20:1-11
22:12-13
22:18-20
23:3

1 Chronicles
4:10
5:20
6:49
11:3
11:18
13:8-10
14:10
14:13-15

15:14,16,29
16:2,4-36
16:37-43
17:16-27
18:11
19:13
21:8-30
22:11-12
23:5
23:13
23:30-31
25:3,7
28:8
29:6-9
29:10-22

2 Chronicles
1:8-11
2:4-6,12
5:11-14
6:1-42
7:4-7
7:12-15
9:8
12:5-8,12
13:14-18
14:11-12
15:1-7,12-15
16:7-9
16:12
18:4-27,31,33-34
20:1-19,21-22,26
23:13,18

29:5,15,20-36
30:15-27
31:2,5-8
32:20-23
32:24-26
33:12-13,15-16,18-19
34:3,20-21,26-28
35:1-19
36:23

Ezra
1:3
2:68-69
6:9-10,12
6:16-17,19-22
7:27-28
8:21-31
8:35
9:3-15
10:1-6,10-14,19

Nehemiah
1:4-11
2:4-8
4:4-5
4:9
5:13
5:19
6:9
6:14
8:6
9:2-38
10:28-30

11:2
11:17
12:24,27,30-31,
38,40,43,46
13:14,22,29-31

Esther
4:3
4:16
9:30-31

Job
1:5
1:20-21
3:1-19
5:1-8
6:8-10
7:7-21
8:5-6
9:1-12,29-33
10:1-22
11:13
13:3,20-28
14:13-22
16:7-21
17:3-4
19:7,25-26
21:14-15
22:21-27
23:3-7
30:20-23
31:35-37
33:26

35:13
38:41
40:1-5
42:1-6
42:7-10

Psalms
3:1-8
4:1-8
5:1-12
6:1-10
7:1-17
8:1-9
9:1-20
10:1-18
11:1-7
12:1-8
13:1-6
14:1-7
15:1-5
16:1-11
17:1-15
18:20-24
18:41
19:1-14
20:1-9
21:1-13
22:1-31
23:1-6
24:1-10
25:1-22
26:1-12
27:1-14

28:1-9	60:1-12	94:1-23
29:1-11	61:1-8	95:1-7
30:1-12	62:1-12	96:1-13
31:1-24	63:1-11	97:1-12
32:1-11	64:1-10	98:1-9
33:1-22	65:1-13	99:1-9
34:1-22	66:1-20	100:1-5
35:1-28	67:1-7	101:1-2
36:5-9	68:1-35	102:1-28
37:1-40	69:1-36	103:1-22
38:1-22	70:1-5	104:1-35
39:1-13	71:1-24	105:1-45
40:1-10	72:1-20	106:1-48
40:11-17	73:1-28	107:1-43
41:1-13	74:1-23	108:1-13
42:1-11	75:1-10	109:1-31
43:1-5	76:1-12	110:1-7
44:1-26	77:1-20	111:1-10
45:1-17	78:1-72	112:1
46:1-11	79:1-13	113:1-9
47:1-9	80:1-19	115:1,17-18
48:1-14	81:1-5	116:1-19
49:1-20	82:1-8	117:1-2
50:1-23	83:1-18	118:1-29
51:1-19	84:1-12	119:1-176
52:1-9	85:1-13	120:1-7
53:1-6	86:1-17	122:1-9
54:1-7	88:1-18	123:1-4
55:1-23	89:1-52	124:1-8
56:1-13	90:1-17	126:1-6
57:1-11	91:1-16	128:5-6
58:1-11	92:1-15	129:1-8
59:1-17	93:1-5	130:1-8

131:1-3
132:1-18
134:1-3
135:1-21
136:1-26
137:1-9
138:1-8
139:1-24
140:1-13
141:1-10
142:1-7
143:1-12
144:1-15
145:1-21
146:1-10
147:1-20
148:1-14
149:1-9
150:1-6

Proverbs
1:28-29
15:8,29
28:9

Ecclesiastes
5:2

Isaiah
1:10-15
7:10-14
12:1-6
25:1-5

26:1-21
27:13
29:13-14
30:18-21
32:11-15
33:1-6
37:4
37:14-22,29-35
38:2-22
53:12
55:6
56:6-7
58:3-14
59:1-2
59:12-15
59:16
60:6
62:6-7
63:7-19
64:1-12
65:24

Jeremiah
7:16
10:6-10
10:23-25
11:14
11:18-23
12:1-4
14:7-9
14:11-12
14:19-22
15:1-9

15:15-18
17:12-18
18:18-23
20:7-18
29:7
29:12-14
31:7
31:9
32:16-27
33:3
33:10-11
36:5-9
37:1-3
42:2-20
43:1-4

Lamentations
1:22
2:19-20
3:8
3:40-44
3:55-66
5:1-22

Ezekiel
8:18
9:8
14:3
14:7-8
14:12-20
20:1-4
22:30
39:27,29

46:13-15

Daniel
2:17-23
3:1-30
4:34-37
6:1-28
9:1-23
10:1-21

Hosea
6:5
7:13-16
8:1-3
11:7
12:4
14:1-3

Joel
1:14
1:19-20
2:17
2:26

2:32

Amos
5:4-7
5:21-27
7:1-9

Jonah
1:5-6
1:14-16
2:1-9
3:5-10
4:1-11

Micah
3:4
3:7
6:6-8
7:7
7:14-20

Habakkuk
1:1-4

1:12-17
3:1-19

Zephaniah
1:4-6
2:3
3:8-10

Zechariah
4:6
7:12-13
8:4-6
8:19-22
10:1
10:6
13:9

Malachi
1:5-9
1:11-14
2:11-14
3:3-4

NEW TESTAMENT

Matthew
2:2
2:11
4:10
5:44
6:5-13

7:7-11
8:2-3
8:5-10
8:24-26
9:2,6-8
9:18-19,23-25

9:20-22
9:27-30
11:25
12:39
14:19
14:23

14:28-31
15:21-28
15:30-31
15:35-36
16:1-4
17:17-20
18:18-20
19:13
20:29-34
21:13
21:18-22
23:39
24:20
26:26-27
26:39-44
27:46
28:9

Mark
1:35
1:40-42
2:4-5,10-12
2:18-20
4:37-40
5:17-19
5:22-23
5:25-34
5:35-42
6:31-32
6:41
6:45-46
7:25-30
7:32-36

8:6-7
8:11-12
8:22-25
9:19-29
10:13-16
10:27
10:46-52
11:9-10
11:17
11:25
12:40
13:18
14:22-23
14:32-39
15:34

Luke
1:10
1:13
1:46-55
1:64
1:67-79
2:13-14
2:20
2:22-24
2:28-35
2:36-38
3:21-22
4:8
4:38-39
4:42
5:12-13
5:16

5:18-20,24-26
5:33-35
6:12-13
6:28
7:2-10
7:16
8:23-25
8:37-39
8:41-42
8:43-48
8:49-55
9:16
9:18
9:28-29
9:41
10:2
10:21-22
11:1-13
12:13-15
13:35
16:19-31
17:5-6
17:12-19
18:1-8
18:9-14
18:27
18:35-43
19:17-40
19:46
20:45-47
21:36
22:19-20
22:31-32

22:39-45
23:34
23:42-43
23:46
23:47
24:30
24:51-53

John
4:23-24
4:46-53
6:11
6:15
6:32-35
9:31
9:35-38
11:22
11:41-47
12:13
12:27-28
14:13-14
14:16
15:7
15:16
16:23-24,
26-27
17:1-26

Acts
1:14
1:24-26
2:42
2:46-47

3:1
4:24-31
6:4
6:6
7:59-60
8:14-15
8:22,24
9:10-12
9:40
10:1-4
10:9
10:30-33
11:5
11:18
12:5,12
13:2-3
14:23
16:13
16:16
16:25
20:36
21:5
22:17
23:11
26:29
27:25
27:35
28:8
28:15

Romans
1:7-10
6:17

7:24-25
8:15
8:26-27
8:34
9:3
10:1
11:2
12:12
14:6
15:30-33
16:25-27

1 Corinthians
1:2-4
7:5
10:30
11:4-5,13
11:24
14:1-19
15:56-57
16:22-24

2 Corinthians
1:2-4
1:10-11
2:14
4:15
8:16
9:10-15
12:8-9
13:7
13:9
13:14

Galatiáns
1:3-5
4:6
6:18

Ephesians
1:2
1:3
1:15-21
2:18
3:12
3:14-21
5:4
5:20
6:18-20

Philippians
1:2-5
1:9-11
1:19
3:1
4:4
4:6
4:19
4:23

Colossians
1:2-4
1:9-12
2:1-2
2:6-7
3:15-17
4:2-4

4:12
4:18

1 Thessalonians
1:1
1:2-3
2:13
3:9-13
5:17-18
5:23-25
5:28

2 Thessalonians
1:2
1:3
1:11-12
2:13
2:16-17
3:1-2
3:5
3:16
3:18

1 Timothy
1:2
1:12-13
1:17
2:1-5
2:8
4:1,3-5
5:5
6:21

2 Timothy
1:2-3
1:16-18
4:16
4:22

Titus
1:4

Philemon
4-6
22
25

Hebrews
2:18
4:15-16
5:7
7:19
7:25
9:24-25
10:12
10:19-22
11:1
11:6
12:28-29
13:3
13:15
13:18
13:20-21
13:25

James
1:5-8
4:2-3
4:8
5:4
5:13-18

1 Peter
1:3
1:17
2:5
3:7
3:12
4:7
4:16
5:7
5:11
5:14

2 Peter
1:2
1:4

3:9
3:18

1 John
1:3,6
1:9
2:1
3:21-22
5:14-16

3 John
2

Jude
2
20-21
24-25

Revelation
1:6-7
1:9
1:17-18

4:8-11
5:8-14
6:9-10
7:9-12
8:3-4
11:6
11:13
11:15-18
12:12
14:2-3
14:6-7
15:2-4
16:2-7
19:1-7
19:10
22:8-9
22:20-21

NOTES

Introduction
1. I have not covered fasting in detail because Ronnie Floyd covered it so thoroughly in his book *The Power of Prayer and Fasting*. Some may wonder why I do not include some of the insights or conclusions about Bible prayer that I include in my oral teaching. Very early, I realized that such expansion would make the book too bulky and might intimidate some readers. Such a large amount of material will available in a later book (God willing).

Chapter 3: Leviticus, Numbers, Deuteronomy
1. For a complete catalog of all the various offerings and sacrifices, see "Offerings and Sacrifices in Bible Times," by W. A. Van Gemeren, in *Evangelical Dictionary of Theology*, ed. Walter A. Elwell (Grand Rapids, MI: Baker, 1984, 2001).

Chapter 7: Psalms, Proverbs, Ecclesiastes, Song of Solomon
1. The classifications define the nature of the kind of parallelism.

Chapter 8: Isaiah, Jeremiah, Lamentations
1. Includes the servant songs in the last half of the book.

Chapter 10: Hosea Through Malachi
1. A superstition occurs when we overstate a truth in such a manner that although its validity is obvious, its importance strikes us as highlighting our discourse.
2. Both Amos and Malachi are concerned with wrong worship. Amos is more concerned with realizing the character of God in worship. Malachi is concerned with insincere worship.

Chapter 11: Matthew, Mark

1. To be discussed later in connection with Matthew 7, Luke 11, and Luke 18.
2. Not to be confused with the earnestness in James 5:16-17.
3. These diseases are listed in many Bible dictionaries.
4. In my treatment of the gospels after Matthew, only cases not treated in previous gospels will be mentioned.

Chapter 12: Luke

1. Those in Matthew and Mark will not be mentioned again.
2. See also Matthew 11:25, which follows the sending of the Twelve.

Chapter 13: John

1. Many discourses in John follow a healing; each discourse would require a book-long explanation.
2. For once, Jesus did not forbid the telling of it; He knew that "his time" had come.
3. John 14–16.

Chapter 14: Acts

1. Where Paul's curse on a sorcerer resulted in the magician's blindness (Acts 13:11).

Chapter 16: Galatians Through Philemon

1. Some of the psalms do as well.

Chapter 17: Hebrews Through Jude

1. See also 1 John 2:1.
2. T. W. Hunt, *Seeing the Unseen* (Colorado Springs, CO: NavPress, 2011), chapter 6 (pages 57–67).
3. Similar to the psalms.

Chapter 18: Revelation

1. The pleasing aroma of the sacrifices is mentioned numerous times throughout the Pentateuch; for example, Genesis 8:21 and Leviticus 23:18.

ABOUT THE AUTHOR

T. W. HUNT is a former prayer specialist with LifeWay Christian Resources and also served on the faculty of Southwestern Baptist Theological Seminary. He is the author of *The Mind of Christ* and a contributor to the *Disciple's Study Bible*. He is coauthor with his daughter, Melana Hunt Monroe, of *The Hope of Glory* (previously published as *From Heaven's View*). Dr. Hunt received his master's and doctoral degrees from the University of North Texas. He lives with his daughter and her family in Conroe, Texas.

More from T. W. Hunt.

Seeing the Unseen
T. W. Hunt

Author and Bible teacher T. W. Hunt directs you to see and hear from God in the supernatural wherever you are — at work, in the kitchen, or on the road.

978-1-61521-581-2

The Hope of Glory
T. W. Hunt and Melana Hunt Monroe

No matter what trials you face, looking at those circumstances from God's perspective will give you a supernatural peace. You'll learn how to grasp this new point of view by focusing on God and His attributes, the Trinity, and spiritual growth.

978-1-61521-732-8

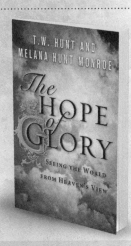

NAVESSENTIALS

Voices of The Navigators—Past, Present, and Future

NavEssentials offer core Navigator messages from Jim Downing, LeRoy Eims, Mike Treneer, and others — at an affordable price. This series will deeply influence generations in the movement of discipleship. Learn from the old and new messages of The Navigators how powerful and transformational the life of a disciple truly is.

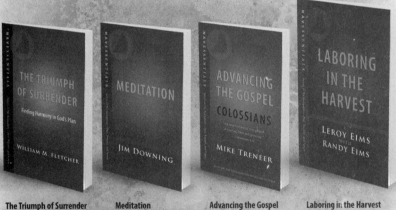

The Triumph of Surrender
by William M. Fletcher
9781615219070 | $5.00

Meditation
by Jim Downing
9781615217250 | $5.00

Advancing the Gospel
by Mike Treneer
9781617471575 | $5.00

Laboring in the Harvest
by LeRoy Eims with Randy Eims
9781615216406 | $10.99

To order, go to **NavPress.com** or call **1-800-366-7788**.

Facebook.com/NavPressPublishing   Twitter.com/NavPress

NAVPRESS
Discipleship Inside Out

Support the Ministry of The Navigators

The Navigators' calling is to advance the gospel of Jesus and His kingdom into the nations through spiritual generations of laborers living and discipling among the lost.

Navigators have invested their lives in people for more than 75 years, coming alongside them life on life to help them passionately know Christ and to make Him known.

The U.S. Navigators' ministry touches lives in varied settings, including college campuses, military bases, downtown offices, urban neighborhoods, prisons, and youth camps.

Dedicated to helping people navigate spiritually, The Navigators aims to make a permanent difference in the lives of people around the world. The Navigators helps its communities of friends to follow Christ passionately and equip them effectively to go out and do the same.

To learn more about donating to The Navigators' ministry,
go to **www.navigators.org/us/support**
or call toll-free at **1-866-568-7827**.